Femininity
AND
Domination

Thinking Gender
Edited by Linda J. Nicholson

Also published in the series

Feminism/Postmodernism
Linda J. Nicholson

Gender Trouble
Judith Butler

Words of Power
Andrea Nye

Femininity AND Domination

STUDIES IN THE PHENOMENOLOGY OF OPPRESSION

Sandra Lee Bartky

ROUTLEDGE New York and London

Published in 1990 by

Routledge
An imprint of Routledge, Chapman and Hall, Inc.
29 West 35 Street
New York, NY 10001

Published in Great Britain by

Routledge
11 New Fetter Lane
London EC4P 4EE

Library of Congress Cataloging in Publication Data

Bartky, Sandra Lee.
    Femininity and domination: studies in the phenomenology of oppression.
      p. cm.—(Thinking gender)
    Includes bibliographical references.
    ISBN 0-415-90185-5—ISBN 0-415-90186-3 (pbk.)
    1. Women—Psychology. 2. Femininity (Psychology) 3. Sex role 4. Patriarchy.
    5. Feminism. I. Title. II. Series.
    HQ1206.B275 1990
    305.42—dc20   90-31568

British Library Cataloguing in Publication Data

Bartky, Sandra Lee
    Femininity and domination: studies in the phenomenology of oppression.—(Thinking gender).
    1. Feminism
    I. Title II. Series
305.42
ISBN 0-415-90185-5
ISBN 0-415-90186-3 pbk

To the memory of my parents,
Ruth Smith Schwartz
and Dr. Harold Schwartz

Contents

Acknowledgments

My work has been nourished from a number of sources, among them the political writings and polemics of the women's movement. But I owe a special debt of gratitude to the Midwest Society for Women in Philosophy, the group to whom many of these papers were first delivered. This philosophical community has attracted an impressive array of counterthinkers and iconoclasts. Considerations of space make it impossible for me to thank them all, though, like the Mormon foremothers of Sonya Johnson, they seem, as I write, to be real and palpable presences, staring down at me from the walls of my study. I can, however, acknowledge the members of this community whose work has, I believe, most directly and immediately influenced my own. Alison Jaggar, very possibly the first thinker ever to entertain the *idea* of a feminist philosophy, showed me very starkly the deficiencies both of liberalism and of orthodox Marxism as well as the androcentrism of much mainstream philosophical ethics; I remain in thrall to her vision of a socialist-feminist society of the future. Iris Young has been engaged too in a radical revision of much Western political theory; she has called into question many received feminist notions as well. Moreover, in a brilliant series of papers on female embodiment, Young demonstrated the power of a phenomenology turned to feminist ends. Alison and Iris, like many other SWIP members, have shown in their own lives the inextricability of theory and practice by demonstrating not only that the writing of feminist theory of the first rank could be combined with political activism but that concrete political work would strengthen and enrich such theory.

Peg Simons, Maria Lugones and Elizabeth Spelman brought me face to face with racism, especially the unintended racism that has infected much feminist writing, including my own. Rhoda Kotzin, Maryellen Symons and I have had many memorable discussions about the relationship of feminist philosophy to the philosophical tradition generally. I was led to think seriously about competition among women by Victoria Davion and about feminist pedagogy and the meaning of collectivity by Ruth Ginzburg. Nancy Fraser woke me from the dogmatic slumbers of modernism to the challenge of postmodernism; I watch with intense interest her application of feminist insights to the critical theory of the welfare state. Marilyn Frye's superbly written and enormously influential critique of patriarchy has set standards of lucidity and stylistic grace for my own work. This is true too of Claudia Card's elegantly constructed and powerfully argued essays in feminist ethics. These standards are hard to meet. The development in this philosophical community of a lesbian perspective in philosophy by Marilyn Frye, Claudia Card, Sarah Hoagland, Jeffner Allen and Joyce Trebilcot (among others) has been a work of remarkable courage as well as a substantial departure not only from traditions in which we were all trained, but from more mainstream feminist philosophy. Exposure to this body of work has often discomfitted me, demanding, as it has, that I examine my own heterosexism. But there are rewards as well: this is philosophical writing that puts me in touch with those feelings of outrage that got me into this in the first place.

Most of those persons already mentioned have offered critiques of one or more of my papers; a few, like Alison Jaggar and Iris Young, of most of them. But there are many other people, both within and without particular feminist philosophical communities who have offered extensive verbal or written critiques of various of my essays. I acknowledge with gratitude their investment of time and energy in my work: Linda Alcoff; Jeffner Allen; Judith Andre; Isaac Balbus; Bat-Ami Bar-On; Marcia Baron; Susan Bordo; Rob Crawford; Dion Farquhar; Ann Ferguson; Judith Gardiner; Ann Garry; Martha Gimenez; Daphne Hampson; Ellin Ringler Henderson; Carole Isaacs; Julia LeSage; Patricia Loose; Martha Pintzuk; Amelie Rorty; David Schweickart; Laurie Shrage; Jan Slagter; Alan Soble; Michael Stocker; the late Irving Thalberg; Thomas Wartenburg; Richard Wasserstrom; Robert Yanal. These critics and commentators may well disagree with many of the ideas I express here, responsibility for which, of course, rests with myself.

I am fortunate to find myself in the unusually collegial Philosophy Department of the University of Illinois at Chicago; this department has encouraged me, over the years, to follow my own philosophical star. I have gotten special help when I needed it, in different ways, from Richard Kraut, our current chair, Neal Grossman, the late Irving Thalberg, and Charlotte Jackson. I owe a special debt of gratitude to the former chair of this department, Ruth Barcan Marcus, who, at a critical moment early in my career, became to me something most needful to a fledgling philosopher: a friend and mentor.

I am privileged to have been part of the UIC Women's Studies Program since its inception: I am especially grateful for the opportunity to do joint work with its staff, in particular with Peg Strobel, the Program's chair, Judith Gardiner, Marilyn Carlander and with students and community women in the Women's Studies Teaching Collective. Marilyn Carlander and I have stormed many a barricade in the ongoing struggle to make our institution more responsive to the needs of women; Marilyn's strength and unwavering commitment have gotten me through many hard times.

A sabbatical leave from my university and a fellowship to the Bunting Institute of Radcliffe College allowed me to complete this project in what can only be described as a utopian setting. I thank the Bunting staff for its consistent support and concrete material assistance.

Linda Nicholson, both friend and academic editor of the Thinking Gender series, offered trenchant critiques of some of these essays. Her own original and historically-oriented approach to feminist theory has been a source of intellectual illumination for me long before this present collaboration. I have been unusually fortunate in my choice of editors: both Linda Nicholson and Maureen MacGrogan, my editor at Routledge, know how to combine the highest standards of professionalism with that encouragement and emotional support which none of us can do without. Maureen, in particular, overcame the diffidence I felt at the prospect of boldly offering my essays, in book form, to the reading public. Finally, let me express to Al Vileisis, my heart's friend and my life's companion, the gratitude I feel for his consistent support of both my theoretical and political commitments.

Note on the Text

Chapters 1 & 3 were first published as articles in Social Theory and Practice, in 1976 and 1982 respectively.

Chapter 2 appeared first as a contribution to *Philosophy and Women*, Wadsworth Publishing, 1979.

Chapter 4 appeared first in Hypatia, Vol. 7, No. 5.

Chapter 5 was a contribution to *Feminism and Foucault: Paths to Resistance*; Quinby & Diamond, eds., Northeastern University Press, 1988.

Chapters 6 & 7 are published here for the first time.

Introduction

The essays in this collection were written over a fifteen-year period. Their composition was labored and difficult; each was separated from the next by a long and sometimes agonized period of waiting during which I thought I would never have another idea. These papers tell of my emergence and development as a feminist thinker and of the way in which my own intellectual odyssey reflects many of the shifting themes and approaches, the preoccupations and controversies, that have characterized feminist philosophical writing since the early seventies.

The two earliest papers were attempts to articulate the profound experience of personal transformation—of "consciousness-raising"—that becoming a feminist meant for women of my generation. "Toward a Phenomenology of Feminist Consciousness," my first essay in philosophy of feminism, tries to record what it is like to undergo such a transformation both in one's own self-understanding and in the understanding one has of the total situation of this self within the social ensemble. My second paper, "On Psychological Oppression," grew out of the shocked discovery of the global and suffocating character of patriarchal culture, again the fruit of consciousness-raising; the attempt in this paper to lay out in some detail the human damage done to women under such a dispensation set the agenda for much of my future work.

Casting about for philosophical resources that might help to understand what was happening to me, I turned to phenomenology, which was not surprising, given my early training in Continental philosophy. But I found the project of classical phenomenology, namely, the analysis of the *a priori* and necessary structures of any possible consciousness, quite useless for my purposes. It was not any possible consciousness I was after, certainly not the "structures" in consciousness of a subject so "pure" as to be elevated above the "mere" determinations of gender and history. I turned instead to an examination of the embodied consciousness of a feminine subject, indeed, of a subject with a

1

specific social and historical location. Simone de Beauvoir had pointed me down this path, though I found her work still dominated by the somewhat ahistorical categories of "self" and "Other."

In "On Psychological Oppression" and in most of the papers to follow, I pay particular attention to those modes of consciousness that can be shown to arise from oppressive intersubjective relationships and which tend at the same time to reproduce and to reaffirm these very relationships: feminine "narcissism" and "masochism"; female shame; sexual self-objectification; loss of self in the sense of merger with another. I examine too those states of consciousness in which older and newer definitions of self are in conflict. I have been interested from the first in the nature of that "femininity" that disempowers us even while it seduces us; I want to understand how the values of a system that oppresses us are able to take up residence inside our minds. While the project of a modest and "situated" phenomenology has never lost its appeal for me, I have taken other conceptual tools where I found them, e.g., from linguistic analysis, Marxism, empirical social science, and psychoanalysis.

"Toward a Phenomenology of Feminist Consciousness" was the easiest paper of all to write. I was impelled to write it not only in order to make sense of what was happening in my own life but because of a practical urgency. I wrote "Phenomenology" as an organizing vehicle for the Society for Women in Philosophy. The society, which had its origin in the Women's Caucus of the American Philosophical Association, met first as an independent and self-standing organization in Chicago in 1971. There were a number of impulses behind the founding of SWIP, not the least of which was our desire to combine our professional identities as philosophers and our new-found identities as feminists. Intense excitement attended the initial meetings of the society. Many of the early participants were not members of the APA. and had never attended a meeting of the Women's Caucus. Most, like myself, had had few if any female colleagues in graduate school and no female teachers. Many had already spent years in profound professional isolation, dealing with an academic sexism that was more blatant then than it is now. A not inconsiderable number were stuck in the kind of dead-end jobs that commonly fell to women philosophers in those days. Many, again like myself, had gotten advanced degrees and were earning a living as teachers of philosophy before they had ever come to know another woman who was earning her living in the same way. We came together in joy and solidarity. We talked all day and most of the night. We stared at one another and even touched each other, as if we were fabulous beasts.

From the start, I understood the depth of my need for this organization. But there was a problem, one that those of us who were charged with the task of setting up programs found particularly acute. To have an organization, of course, one needed programs. But to have the sort of organization we envisioned, we would need programs that somehow combined feminism and philosophy. But how? There was precious little of anything around that one could call "feminist philosophy." Indeed, given the conceptions of philosophy that we had learned in graduate school—conceptions that still largely hold sway—it wasn't entirely clear how philosophy could continue to be philosophy and yet become feminist. Philosophy was concerned with matters transcendental, with being *qua* being and perception *per se*. What had our concerns to do with these? Clearly, if there were to be such a thing as feminist philosophy, we who were philosophers and feminists would have to invent it. "Phenomenology" was my contribution to this invention. By writing it, I created one more program slot, making it a little more likely that there would be one more program; in this way I did what I could to keep this precious but still fragile organization alive. Today, the Society for Women in Philosophy has three national divisions, several smaller regional groups, and its own journal, *Hypatia*. It has inspired the organizing of similar societies in a number of other countries. The U.S. and, later, the Canadian Society for Women in Philosophy became the central organizational vehicles for the development of English-language feminist philosophy.

Much early feminist philosophy was taken up with the articulation and defense of what might be called a "paradigm-shift," i.e., the emergence of radically new visions of self and society. Having consolidated its ground, feminist philosophy was then free to examine more specific problems. My own work follows this general tendency. "Narcissism, Femininity, and Alienation" reflects the long and troubled pursuit of a synthesis of Marxism and feminism that occupied many feminist philosophers (and feminist thinkers in other fields as well) during much of the seventies and well into the eighties. While a rich and complex body of theory developed around the question of such a synthesis, the whole discussion proved inconclusive and has since become unfashionable. I am disheartened by the decline of interest among feminists in Marxist theory, for I consider Marxism to be the most complex and intellectually sophisticated body of theory to date on the nature of class relations and the mechanisms of class oppression. Gender oppression cannot be understood in isolation from class oppression. Nor, in my view, can racial oppression, an understanding of which is also crucial to a theory of gender oppression. The turning away from a serious theoretical interest in class, hence, in the possibility of constructing a more just society, bespeaks, in my view, a failure of hope. The visionary and utopian impulse that animated both the New Left and the early women's movement has receded before the growing tide of conservatism. As I write this, the current prospects for any kind of significant reform seem dim. The women's movement and the black liberation movement are struggling just to keep whatever gains they were able to make in a more progressive period. The fashionable poststructuralist attack on the kind of "totalizing" theory that Marxist and socialist feminists were trying to construct in the days of the Marxism-feminism debate is, in my view, a symptom of the same political malaise. As I write this, I realize that my own work too has followed the fashion, that I have not been immune to the prevailing pessimism, that my choice of topics has been controlled, far more than I realized and more than I wished, by an anticipation of what would interest my audience and that this anticipation prevailed, even in the face of some disquiet about the direction of that interest.

"Feminine Masochism and the Politics of Personal Transformation" was my contribution to the various feminist "sex wars," those that were waged first between lesbian separatists and nonseparatist feminists, later between "libertarian" and anti-pornography feminists. "Foucault, Femininity, and the Modernization of Patriarchal Power" is an attempt to appropriate certain insights of poststructuralism—a tendency that now dominates feminist literary theory and that is gaining increasing influence among feminist philosophers as well—for a philosophy of female embodiment. Even though I myself have been much influenced by these newer tendencies, I try in the last paper in the volume, "Feeding Egos and Tending Wounds: Deference and Disaffection in Women's Emotional Labor," to salvage some Marxist categories of analysis from the depredations of feminist poststructuralism; at the same time my critique of women's care giving in this paper is an attempt to join the continuing philosophical discussion about the possibility of a feminist ethics of care, an ethics grounded in women's traditions of nurturance that would replace a purportedly masculinist ethics of rights and rules.

But from the start, I meant these papers to be more than mere theoretical excursions or "interesting" contributions to current debates; I intended them to be political interventions as well. Most of my writing is meant to offer occasions for consciousness-raising, thought by many to be the most effective political practice of the women's movement. I hoped that "Toward a Phenomenology of Feminist Consciousness" would explain to nonfeminists, or not-yet feminists, what we were about; indeed, I was trying to seduce them. In my two papers on the female body, "Narcissism, Femininity, and Alienation" and "Foucault, Femininity, and the Modernization of Patriarchal Power," I invite women to consider the effect upon ourselves of that relentless self-objectification to which we have been condemned by the current norms of feminine bodily acceptability. In "Shame and Gender," I encourage women to reflect upon the ways in which the most ordinary kinds of interpersonal situations can be profoundly damaging to our self-esteem and how this subtle undermining can go on, surprisingly, behind our backs. In "Feeding Egos and Tending Wounds," I offer women the occasion to consider some of the subtler ways in which we may be disempowered by the current division of emotional labor whereby we end up giving more emotional support to men than they give us in return. I am trying to get women angry. More precisely put, I am trying to give women permission to feel the anger that I believe is already there. Clearly, the audience I have in mind in these papers is female. But some of my best readers have been men. There are fair-minded men around too, more than a few, and I have been gratified by the many men who have valued my work. I have tried never to stray too far from the realities of everyday life and, wherever possible, to avoid technical jargon, though the desire to impress professional audiences sometimes got the better of me. Of all the charges that are brought against philosophy, how rarely does anyone say that much of it is boring. I have tried, above all, not to be boring.

I intended many of these papers not only as general consciousness-raising vehicles but as active interventions in the discourse and politics of the women's movement itself. So, in "Narcissism, Femininity, and Alienation," "On Psychological Oppression," and "Feeding Egos and Tending Wounds," I try to exhibit to non-Marxist, even anti-Marxist feminists—women whom I respect and with whom I have worked politically—the power of Marxist ideas; once again, I am trying to practice seduction. But several of these papers (especially "Foucault, Femininity, and the Modernization of Patriarchal Power") are critical of orthodox Marxism, too, and certainly of the prevailing liberal feminism: I argue in many places that a feminist reconstruction of self and society must go far beyond anything now contemplated in the theory or politics of the mainstream women's movement. I recognize (especially in "Foucault, Femininity, and the Modernization of Patriarchal Power") that the mere contemplation of this reconstruction generates a level of anxiety which must itself be interrogated, for it reveals the extent to which the established order of domination has taken root within our very identities.

When I began writing "Feminine Masochism and the Politics of Personal Transformation," I thought that I would be able to exhibit "feminine masochism," like the self-objectification I examined in the paper on narcissism, as a species of alienation. But I found myself unable to do this and so had to abandon (but perhaps not forever) the project of the "totalizing" feminist theory of alienation on which I believed I was then at work. Instead, the paper went its own way and began to generate its own logic. It can be read as an intervention, too, this time in the theory and politics both of lesbian separatism, and of the feminist anti-pornography movement. While I treat neither one very explicitly, preferring a more oblique approach, I argue that the call for a politically correct sexuality, which is of course central to both movements, is ill-conceived and divisive. Even "Toward a Phenomenology of Feminist Consciousness" can be read as an intervention of a sort, for here I remind a movement that was factionalized almost from the start what we feminists have in common, what it was like to undergo those alterations in consciousness that led us to the very terrain we sometimes dispute so bitterly.

I have never agreed with those feminists who think that we can set patriarchal thought aside in its entirety and construct *de novo* a philosophy based on women's daily realities or, as some French feminists have suggested, on the specificities of female embodiment. Philosophical reflection—indeed, any reflection—is always already rooted in some inherited schema or, as is more commonly said today, in some *text;* these texts are bound to be class-, race-, and gender-biased. Hence, we must approach our tradition with deep suspicion; we must test its claims against our own hard-won insights; we must sort and sift among its materials to see what we can use and what we must discard.

My own attitude toward the philosophical tradition in which I was trained, and toward the history of philosophy generally, is deeply ambivalent, much like the troubled relationship some children have toward their parents. I feel toward the tradition a mixture of gratitude and resentment. I am grateful for the idea of intellectual rigor I got from philosophical training and for the opportunity to reflect with some intelligence on the nature and meaning of my own experience. My life would have been greatly impoverished had I never been exposed to the boldness and grandeur of the great speculative systems. I am grateful too for whatever wisdom I have been able to find in philosophical texts, though I haven't found much and I haven't found it often. On the other hand, I deeply resent the way in which, with few exceptions, women have been insulted and debased by traditional philosophy or else just rendered invisible. I take seriously the argument that philosophy in the West has been dominated by conceptual hierarchies that are covertly gender-coded. Here then is another story my papers tell—of my long, laborious, inconclusive, and continuing effort to come to terms with the parent tradition.

In some papers, I draw upon the resources of this tradition, using, e.g., the Sartrian notion of "the gaze" to illuminate the nature of sexual objectification; the Marxist conception of alienation to describe, also to condemn, the processes of feminine self-objectification; Foucault's account of "disciplinary practices" to understand certain crucial dimensions of the constitution of embodied femininity. At the same time, I have tried to expose the phallocentrism in our tradition that has taken up residence even in its most stirring discourses of emancipation. I am at war throughout with the principal personage of traditional philosophy, that abstract subject who masquerades as everyone and anyone, but is really a male subject in disguise.

At the same time, I make in these papers what I hope are genuine contributions to philosophy. In "On Psychological Oppression," I find the concept of oppression as it is standardly employed in political philosophy narrow and inadequate; I argue for a richer and more complex notion. In "Narcissism, Femininity, and Alienation," I implicitly critique but try at the same time to extend the range of the powerful concept of alienation. In "Feminine Masochism and the Politics of Personal Transformation," I argue that sexual fantasy, not just sexual behavior, should be made the object of moral evaluation; I argue, equally vigorously, that this evaluation should not, indeed cannot, take the form of a narrow moralism. Philosophical ethics has largely ignored fantasy, relegating it to the sphere of the "private" where, it is presumed, moral predicates cannot be applied. But the feminist denial of the conventional distinction between public and private spheres, as well as the challenge posed by radical feminist critiques of contemporary sexuality, should, it seems to me, put the issue of fantasy squarely on the philosophical agenda. When I contemplate the silence in which mainstream ethics has wrapped this touchy issue, I am uneasy: Is there something here that won't bear scrutiny? "Feeding Egos and Tending Wounds" is an implicit critique of philosophical ethics as well: I point here to a rich and complex field both of human relationship and of intra-subjective experience that mainstream moral philosophy has just ignored. In "Shame and Gender," I invade the terrain of analytic moral psychology, arguing that this branch of philosophy has given us an incomplete, excessively intellectualistic, and somewhat self-serving account of this powerful emotion of self-assessment.

These, then, are the several themes that tie together the papers in this collection: the address to activists; the critique and revision of traditional philosophical discourse; the attempt to turn that discourse to feminist ends. Most of my papers cast our gender arrangements and their effects in a highly critical light. Hence, they focus not on what is positive in women's experience, but on what is not, on characteristically feminine anxieties, fear, and obsessions: in a word, on the internalization of pervasive intimations of inferiority. Women's joys and triumphs are not my theme. I realize that this may give the collection as a whole a rather pessimistic cast. But this is not the whole story. Theoretical work done in the service of political ends may exhibit a "pessimism of the intellect," but the point of doing such work at all is that "optimism of the will" without which any serious political commitment is impossible. It is an immeasurable political advance to break out of that suffocating consensus that denies or trivializes our complaints. It is crucial too to describe with some accuracy the way things appear to us—a project that requires, often as not, that we contest the offical story about how things are *supposed* to appear.

I have sometimes been charged with defeatism because I have avoided prescription in my writing in favor of analysis and description. I do this because I find "what is to be done" either too obvious or else not at all obvious. Let me explain. On the one hand, much of what I decry is so deeply rooted both in our culture and in our own interior lives that a few prescriptive paragraphs tacked onto the end of a paper would be fatuous–or presumptuous. On the other hand, the women's movement has already generated a good deal of practice around much of what gets discussed here in theory. So, for example, the connection between the remedies that have been developed to combat sexual harassment at work and the sexual objectification I scrutinize in "On Psychological Oppression" seemed to me too obvious to mention.

In the *Nicomachean Ethics,* Aristotle admits that strict proof is impossible in matters of morals (and presumably in political matters as well); hence, the philosopher who enters upon this domain must be content to speak about "things which are only for the most part true," never upon things that are invariably and necessarily true.[1] Given the extreme diversity of women as a group, I hope I have gotten this far. While my papers are certainly over-generalized (because constant qualification would make it impossible to say anything at all), I hope it is clear from their context that I am not treating of things that are invariably true of women in all times and places, only of what is currently for the most part true for women in advanced industrial society. The papers that deal with dilemmas in the transition to feminism are clearly not about all women, though I hope they have something to say to women in our society generally. Nor is the "chauvinized" woman who appears so frequently in these papers—ashamed, eager to please, worried about her weight—meant to be an accurate portrait of Everywoman either. But I sketch this woman over and over, not only because there is much of her in me and in many other women as well, but because her desire reflects the current social norms according to which female desire is, or is supposed to be, constituted. We are supposed to desire as she desires; if we don't, others may punish us; or else, feeling guilty, we may punish ourselves. I know too that most women in the world do not live in advanced industrial societies. Nevertheless, as their societies "develop," women in other countries are subject to norms (including gender norms) and to practices (e.g., the beauty contest) that come increasingly to resemble our own.

The introspective method I so often employ carries with it both clear advantages and major risks. When I came to reread my earlier work, I was shocked to find passages in my first two papers that betrayed a certain racism. I, a white woman with a long history of commitment to the civil rights movement, had, without knowing what I was doing, made the experience of women of color marginal, of white women central. I thought at the time that I was just writing about "women." I have revised the few passages in "Toward a Phenomenology of Feminist Consciousness" that display this unintended racism; "On Psychological Oppression" required more extensive rewriting, though I have tried to keep intact the main idea of the paper, namely, the attempt to use Frantz Fanon's analysis of the psychological effects of colonialism to lay bare some psychological effects of sexism. (Except in these first two essays, I have not attempted to bring my source citations up to date.)

I try to be careful now and suspicious of myself, to look and see, to go and ask. Since entering upon this hermeneutic of suspicion, I have found out how little is known about differences in women's interior lives. When I wrote "Feminine Masochism and the Politics of Personal Transformation," for example, I was not able to discern from the scanty literature on the topic whether women's sexual fantasies varied by race, social class, or family type. When I began reading for "Foucault, Femininity, and the Modernization of Patriarchal Power," I was curious to learn whether adolescent black, brown, or Asian girls from similar socioeconomic backgrounds were as likely as white girls to develop anorexia nervosa, but once again I found no answers in the available empirical literature. More research would be very fine indeed, but it is no more the answer to this problem than are "good intentions" on the part of privileged women. The current imbalances will persist until the maldistribution of every social good, including the means of interpretation and communication, is ended; then every woman who wishes to can speak for herself.

It would be arrogant to claim that I have or ever could be entirely successful in purging my writing of every vestige of race and class privilege. A certain privilege is already reflected in my very choice of themes: A woman who had known material deprivation in a way I never have might well have chosen to deal with issues that were linked more centrally to poverty. Even though I stand behind my critique of the kind of "standard" heterosexual relationship that comes under scrutiny in "Feedings Egos and Tending Wounds," I know full well that many single mothers, struggling to survive on a single paycheck, would like nothing better than to enter upon such a relationship. But I have tried, with increasing urgency and growing self-awareness, to say nothing that I knew to be generally false of women of other racial and economic groups. It seems to me that many of the themes that weave in and out of these papers speak to women of many conditions—women who are lesbian and women who are not, women of color and white women, poor women and privileged women. All sorts of women have known in their daily lives the low self-esteem that is attendant upon cultural depreciation, the humiliation of sexual objectification, the troubled relationship to a socially inferiorized body, the confusions and even the anguish that come in the wake of incompatible social definitions of womanhood; women of all kinds and colors have endured not only the overt, but also the disguised and covert attacks of a misogynist society.

The philosophical myth of the abstract subject is accompanied by another myth, one almost as widespread, namely, the idea that Mind itself, abstract cogitation, and nothing in a philosopher's life determines what is "philosophically interesting." On this view, philosophy is just a kind of puzzle and philosophers, when they do philosophy, are not persons of flesh and blood who love and suffer but merely minds thinking. Once, I too wanted to be a mind thinking; like many other philosophers, I was drawn to philosophy by Plato's promise that I could become the "spectator of all time and all existence."[2] But it didn't work. The vicissitudes of ordinary existence kept coming between me and the Absolute. My own being came to interest me more than being *qua* being.

I too have pursued the philosophically interesting and the theoretically puzzling. But I have mined my own fears and anxieties as well, drawn upon my own consciousness, indeed, the most chauvinized aspects of this consciousness, as a resource for theory. Topics that would have required the tapping of a fund of experience I myself have never had (such as motherhood) I have avoided. But what I have written is not a confession, either. Much of myself, perhaps most of myself, is not here at all. Often I extrapolate from very little or else exaggerate what are no more than mere tendencies in my own conscious life— this in order to "fix" the phenomena and to allow them to come forward with more clarity. I have bestowed a certain level of ideality on the modes of awareness I choose to examine. I purge them of extraneous features, of moments of boredom or resistance, again in order to fix them better. Hence, I do not claim in their entirety the states of consciousness that are herein examined. But I do not disclaim them either. They are, after all, what I chose to study, some, like certain obsessional, though "normal," modes of embodied consciousness in women, more than once. Here, perhaps, is the final tale these papers tell—a tale of the philosopher become exorcist of her own demons.

1

Toward a Phenomenology of Feminist Consciousness

Contemporary feminism has many faces. The best attempts so far to deal with the scope and complexity of the movement have divided feminists along ideological lines. Thus, liberal, Marxist, neo-Marxist, and what are called "radical" feminists differ from one another in that they have differing sets of beliefs about the origin and nature of sexism and thus quite different prescriptions for the proper way of eliminating it. But this way of understanding the nature of the women's movement, however, indispensable, is not the only way. While I would not hesitate to call someone a feminist who supported a program for the liberation of women and who held beliefs about the nature of contemporary society appropriate to such a political program, something crucial to an understanding of feminism is overlooked if its definition is so restricted.

To be a feminist, one has first to become one. For many feminists, this involves the experience of a profound personal transformation, an experience which goes far beyond that sphere of human activity we regard ordinarily as "political." This transforming experience, which cuts across the ideological divisions within the women's movement, is complex and multifaceted. In the course of undergoing the transformation to which I refer, the feminist changes her *behavior*: She makes new friends; she responds differently to people and events; her habits of consumption change; sometimes she alters her living arrangements or, more dramatically, her whole style of life. She may decide to pursue a career, to develop potentialities within herself which had long lain dormant or she may commit herself to political struggle. In a biting and deliberately flat tone, one feminist enumerates some of the changes in her own life:

During the past year I . . . was arrested on a militant women's liberation

11

action, spent some time in jail, stopped wearing makeup and shaving my legs, started learning Karate and changed my politics completely.[1]

These changes in behavior go hand in hand with changes in *consciousness*: to become a feminist is to develop a radically altered consciousness of oneself, of others, and of what, for lack of a better term, I shall call "social reality."[2] Feminists themselves have a name for the struggle to clarify and to hold fast to this way of apprehending things: They call it "consciousness-raising." A "raised" consciousness on the part of women is not only a causal factor in the emergence of the feminist movement itself but also an important part of its political program. Many small discussion groups exist solely for the purpose of consciousness-raising. But what happens when one's consciousness is raised? What is a fully developed feminist consciousness like? In this paper, I would like to examine not the full global experience of liberation, involving as it does new ways of being as well as new ways of perceiving, but, more narrowly, those distinctive ways of perceiving which characterize feminist consciousness. What follows will be a highly tentative attempt at a morphology of feminist consciousness. Without claiming to have discovered them all, I shall try to identify some structural features of that altered way of apprehending oneself and the world which is both product and content of a raised consciousness. But before I begin, I would like to make some very general remarks about the nature of this consciousness and about the conditions under which it emerges.

Although the oppression of women is universal, feminist consciousness is not. While I am not sure that I could demonstrate the necessity of its appearance in this time and place and not in another, I believe it is possible to identify two features of current social reality which, if not sufficient, are at least necessary conditions for the emergence of feminist consciousness. These features constitute, in addition, much of the content of this consciousness. I refer, first, to the existence of what Marxists call "contradictions" in our society and, second, to the presence, due to these same contradictions, of concrete circumstances which would permit a significant alteration in the status of women.

In Marxist theory, the stage is set for social change when existing forms of social interaction—property relations as well as values, attitudes, and beliefs—come into conflict with new social relations which are generated by changes in the mode of production:

> At a certain stage of their development, the material forces of production in society come in conflict with the existing relations of production or—what is but a legal expression for the same thing—with the property relations within which they had been at work before. From forms of development of the forces of production these relations turn into their fetters. Then comes the period of social revolution.[3]

Social conflict regularly takes an ideological form, so much so that conflicts which are fundamentally economic in origin may appear to be struggles between ideas, as, for instance, between competing conceptions of the nature of legitimate political authority or of woman's proper sphere. To date, no one has offered a comprehensive analysis of those changes in the socioeconomic structure of contemporary American society which have made possible the emergence of feminist consciousness.[4] This task is made doubly difficult by the fact that these changes constitute no completed process, no convenient object for dispassionate historical investigation, but are part of the fluid set of circumstances in which each of us must find our way from one day to another and whose ultimate direction is as yet unclear. In spite of this, several features of current social reality cannot escape notice.

First, if we add to the Marxist notion of "modes of production" the idea of "modes of (biological) reproduction," then it is evident that the development of cheap and efficient types of contraception has been instrumental in changing both the concrete choices women are able to make and the prevailing conceptions about woman's function and destiny. Second, the rapid growth of service industries has had much to do with the steady rise in the percentage of women in the work force, since the post–World War II low in the early fifties. While poor women and women of color have often had to work for wages, middle-class women were largely restricted to the roles of wife, mother, and home-maker; this restriction, together with the rationales that justify it, is clearly out of phase with the entry of millions of such women into the market economy. The growth and spread of a technology to ease the burden of housekeeping, a technology which is itself the result of a need on the part of late capitalism for "innovations" in production, serves further to undermine traditional conceptions about woman's place. During part of the period of the most rapid rise in the percentage of women in the work force, to cite still another "contradiction," there appeared an anomalous and particularly virulent form of the "feminine mystique," which, together with its companion, the ideal of "togetherness," had the effect, among other things, of insuring that the family would remain an efficient vehicle of consumption.[5] What triggered feminist consciousness most immediately, no doubt, were the civil rights movement and the peace and student movements of the sixties; while they had other aims as well, the latter movements may also be read as expressions of protest against the growing bureaucratization, depersonalization, and inhumanity of late capitalist society. Women often found themselves forced to take subordinate positions within these movements; it did not take long for them to see the contradiction between the oppression these movements were fighting in the larger society and their own continuing oppression in the life of these movements themselves.[6]

Clearly, any adequate account of the "contradictions" of late capitalism, that is, of the conflicts, the instabilities, the ways in which some parts of the social whole are out of phase with others, would be a complex and elaborate task. But whatever a complete account of these contradictions would look like, it is essential to understand as concretely as possible how the contradictory factors we are able to identify are lived and suffered by particular people. The facts of economic development are crucial to an understanding of any phenomenon of social change, but they are not the phenomenon in its entirety. Dogmatic Marxists have regarded consciousness as a mere reflection of material conditions and therefore uninteresting as an object for study in and of itself. Even Marxist scholars of a more humane cast of mind have not paid sufficient attention to the ways in which the social and economic tensions they study are played out in the lives of concrete individuals. There is an anguished consciousness, an inner uncertainty and confusion which characterizes human subjectivity in periods of social change—and I shall contend that feminist consciousness, in large measure, is an anguished consciousness—of whose existence Marxist scholars seem largely unaware. Indeed, the only sort of consciousness which is discussed with any frequency in the literature is "class consciousness," a somewhat unclear idea whose meaning Marxists themselves dispute. In sum, then, the incorporation of phenomenological methods into Marxist analysis is necessary, if the proper dialectical relations between human consciousness and the material modes of production are ever to be grasped in their full concreteness.

Women have long lamented their condition, but a lament, pure and simple, need not be an expression of feminist consciousness. As long as their situation is apprehended as natural, inevitable, and inescapable, women's consciousness of themselves, no matter how alive to insult and inferiority, is not yet feminist consciousness. This consciousness, as I contended earlier, emerges only when there exists a genuine possibility for the partial or total liberation of women. This possibility is more than a mere accidental accompaniment of feminist consciousness; rather, feminist consciousness is the apprehension of that possibility. The very *meaning* of what the feminist apprehends is illuminated by the light of what ought to be. The given situation is first understood in terms of a state of affairs in which what is given would be negated and radically transformed. To say that feminist consciousness is the experience in a certain way of certain specific contradictions in the social order is to say that the feminist apprehends certain features of social reality as intolerable, as to be rejected in behalf of a transforming project for the future. "It is on the day that we can conceive of a different state of affairs that a new light falls on our troubles and we *decide* that these are unbearable."[7] What Sartre would call her "transcendence," her project of negation and transformation, makes possible what are specifically feminist ways of apprehending contradictions in the social order. Women workers who are not feminists know that they receive unequal pay for equal work, but they may think that the arrangement is just; the feminist sees this situation as an instance of exploitation and an occasion for struggle. Feminists are no more aware of different things than other people; they are aware of the same things differently. Feminist consciousness, it might be ventured, turns a "fact" into a "contradiction"; often, features of social reality are first apprehended *as* contradictory, as in conflict with one another, or as disturbingly out of phase with one another, from the vantage point of a radical project of transformation.

Thus, we understand what we are and where we are in the light of what we are not yet. But the perspective from which I understand the world must be rooted in the world too. My comprehension of what I and my world can become must take account of what we are. The possibility of a transformed society which allows the feminist to grasp the significance of her current situation must somehow be contained in the apprehension of her current situation: the contradictory situation in which she finds herself she perceives as unstable, as carrying within itself the seeds of its own dissolution. There is no way of telling, by a mere examination of some form of consciousness, whether the possibilities it incorporates are realizable or not; this depends on whether the situation is such as to contain within itself the sorts of material conditions which will bring to fruition a human expectation. If no such circumstances are present, then the consciousness in question is not the kind of consciousness which accompanies a genuine political project at all, but merely fantasy. I think that an examination of the circumstances of our lives will show that feminist consciousness and the radical project of transformation which animates it is, if less than an absolutely certain anticipation of what must be, more than mere fantasy.

The relationship between consciousness and concrete circumstances can best be described as "dialectical". Feminist consciousness is more than a mere reflection of external material conditions, for the transforming and negating perspective which it incorporates first allows these conditions to be revealed *as* the conditions they are. But on the other hand, the apprehension of some state of affairs as intolerable, as to-be-transformed, does not, in and of itself, transform it.

II

Feminist consciousness is consciousness of *victimization*. To apprehend oneself as victim is to be aware of an alien and hostile force outside of oneself which is responsible for the blatantly unjust treatment of women and which enforces a stifling and oppressive system of sex-role differentiation. For some feminists, this hostile power is "society" or "the system"; for others, it is simply men. Victimization is impartial, even though its damage is done to each one of us personally. One is victimized as a woman, as one among many. In the realization that others are made to suffer in the same way I am made to suffer lies the beginning of a sense of solidarity with other victims. To come to see oneself as victim, to have such an altered perception of oneself and of one's society is not to see things in the same old way while merely judging them differently or to superimpose new attitudes on things like frosting a cake.

The consciousness of victimization is immediate and revelatory; it allows us to discover what social reality is really like.

The consciousness of victimization is a divided consciousness. To see myself as victim is to know that I have already sustained injury, that I live exposed to injury, that I have been at worst mutilated, at best diminished in my being. But at the same time, feminist consciousness is a joyous consciousness of one's own power, of the possibility of unprecedented personal growth and the release of energy long suppressed. Thus, feminist consciousness is both consciousness of weakness and consciousness of strength. But this division in the way we apprehend ourselves has a positive effect, for it leads to the search both for ways of overcoming those weaknesses in ourselves which support the system and for direct forms of struggle against the system itself.

The consciousness of victimization may be a consciousness divided in a second way. The awareness I have of myself as victim may rest uneasily alongside the awareness that I am also and at the same time enormously privileged, more privileged than the overwhelming majority of the world's population. I myself enjoy both white-skin privilege and the privileges of comparative affluence. In our society, of course, women of color are not so fortunate; white women, as a group and on average, are substantially more economically advantaged than many persons of color, especially women of color; white women have better housing and education, enjoy lower rates of infant and maternal mortality, and, unlike many poor persons of color, both men and women, are rarely forced to live in the climate of street violence that has become a standard feature of urban poverty. But even women of color in our society are relatively advantaged in comparison to the appalling poverty of women in, e.g., Africa and Latin America.

Many women do not develop a consciousness divided in this way at all: they see themselves, to be sure, as victims of an unjust system of social power, but they remain blind to the extent to which they themselves are implicated in the victimization of others. What this means is that the "raising" of a woman's consciousness is, unfortunately, no safeguard against her continued acquiescence in racism, imperialism, or class oppression. Sometimes, however, the entry into feminist consciousness, for white women especially, may bring in its wake a growth in political awareness generally: The disclosure of one's own oppression may lead to an understanding of a range of misery to which one was heretofore blind.

But consciousness divided in this way may tend, just as easily, to produce confusion, guilt, and paralysis in the political sphere. To know oneself as a "guilty victim" is to know oneself as *guilty*; this guilt is sometimes so profound that it sets a woman up for political manipulation. When this happens, she may find herself caught up in political agendas or even in political organizations that speak only to her guilt and not, at the same time, to her need; indeed, she may have been recruited on the basis of her guilt alone. The awakening comes at last: The recognition that she has been manipulated—"guilt-tripped"—brings in its wake resentment, anger, and very often a headlong and permanent refusal to engage ever again in any political activity. A consciousness so divided, again, so guilt-ridden, may experience paralysis in still another way: Trained anyhow to subordinate her needs to the needs of others, a woman may be so over-whelmed by the discovery of her own complicity in such evils as racism or imperialism that she denies herself permission fully to confront the real discom-forts of her own situation. Her anger is mobilized on behalf of everyone else, but never on her own behalf. We all know women like this, admirable women who toil ceaselessly in the vineyards of social justice, alive to the insults borne by others, but seemingly oblivious to the ones meant for them.

To apprehend myself as victim in a sexist society is to know that there are few places where I can hide, that I can be attacked almost anywhere, at any time, by virtually anyone. Innocent chatter, the currency of ordinary social life, or a compliment ("You don't think like a woman"), the well-intentioned advice of psychologists, the news item, the joke, the cosmetics advertisement—none of these is what it is or what it was. Each reveals itself, depending on the circumstances in which it appears, as a threat, an insult, an affront, as a re-minder, however, subtle, that I belong to an inferior caste. In short, these are revealed as instruments of oppression or as articulations of a sexist institution. Since many things are not what they seem to be and since many apparently harmless sorts of things can suddenly exhibit a sinister dimension, social reality is revealed as *deceptive*.

Contemporary thinkers as diverse as Heidegger and Marcuse have written about the ambiguity and mystification which are so prominent a feature of contemporary social life. Feminists are alive to one certain dimension of a society which seems to specialize in duplicity—the sexist dimension. But the deceptive nature of this aspect of social reality itself makes the feminist's experi-ence of life, her anger and sense of outrage difficult to communicate to the insensitive or uninitiated; it increases her frustration and reinforces her isola-tion. There is nothing ambiguous about racial segregation or economic discrimi-nation. It is far less difficult to point to such abuses than it is to show how, for example, the "tone" of a news story can transform a piece of reportage into a refusal to take women's political struggles seriously. The male reporter for a large local daily paper who described the encounter of Betty Friedan and the Republican Women's Caucus at Miami never actually used the word "fish-wife," nor did he say outright that the political struggles of women are worthy of ridicule; he merely chose to describe the actions of the individuals involved in such a way as to make them appear ridiculous. (Nor, it should be added, did he fail to describe Ms. Friedan as "petite.") It is difficult to characterize the tone of an article, the patronizing implications of a remark, the ramifications of some accepted practice, and it is even more difficult to describe what it is like to be bombarded ten or a hundred times daily with these only half-submerged weapons of a sexist system. This, no doubt, is one reason why, when trying to make a case for feminism, we find ourselves referring almost exclusively to the "hard data" of discrimination, like unequal pay, rather than to those pervasive intimations of inferiority which may rankle at least as much.

Many people know that things are not what they seem to be. The feminist knows that the thing revealed in its truth at last will, likely as not, turn out to be a thing which threatens or demeans. But however unsettling it is to have to find one's way about in a world which dissimulates, it is worse not to be able to determine the nature of what is happening at all. Feminist consciousness is often afflicted with category confusion, an inability to know how to classify things. For instance, is the timidity I display at departmental meetings merely my own idiosyncrasy and personal shortcoming, an effect of factors which went into the development of my personality uniquely, or is it a typically female trait, a shared inability to display aggression, even verbal aggression? Why is the suggestion I make ignored? Is it intrinsically unintelligent, or is it because I am a woman and therefore not to be taken seriously? The persistent need I have to make myself "attractive," to fix my hair and put on lipstick—is it the false need of a "chauvinized" woman, encouraged since infancy to identify her human value with her attractiveness in the eyes of men, or does it express a basic need to affirm a wholesome love for one's body by adorning it, a behavior common in primitive societies, allowed us but denied to men in our own still puritan culture? Uncertainties such as these make it difficult to decide how to struggle and whom to struggle against, but the very possibility of understanding one's own motivations, character traits, and impulses is also at stake. In sum, feminists suffer what might be called a "*double ontological shock*": first, the realization that what is really happening is quite different from what appears to be happening, and, second, the frequent inability to tell what is really happening at all.

Since discriminatory sex-role differentiation is a major organizing principle of our society, the list of its carriers and modes of communication would be unending. The sorts of things already mentioned were chosen at random. Little political, professional, educational, or leisure-time activity is free of the blight of sexism. Startlingly few personal relationships exist without it. Feminist consciousness is a little like paranoia, especially when the feminist first begins to apprehend the full extent of sex discrimination and the subtlety and variety of the ways in which it is enforced. Its agents are everywhere, even inside her own mind, since she can fall prey to self-doubt or to a temptation to compliance. In response to this, the feminist becomes vigilant and suspicious. Her apprehension of things, especially of direct or indirect communication with other people is characterized by what I shall call "*wariness*." Wariness is anticipation of the possibility of attack, of affront or insult, of disparagement, ridicule, or the hurting blindness of others. It is a mode of experience which anticipates experience in a certain way; it is an apprehension of the inherently threatening character of established society. While it is primarily the established order of things of which the feminist is wary, she is wary of herself, too. She must be always on the alert lest her pervasive sense of injury provoke in her without warning some public display of emotion, such as violent weeping, which she would rather suppress entirely or else endure in private. Many feminists are perpetually wary lest their own anger be transformed explosively into aggressive or hostile behavior of the sort which would be imprudent or even dangerous to display.

Some measure of wariness is a constant in feminist experience, but the degree to which it is present will be a function of other factors in a feminist's life— her level of political involvement, perhaps, the extent of her exploration of the social milieu, or the extent to which she allows resignation or humor to take away the sting. Characteristic of this kind of consciousness too is the *alteration* of a heightened awareness of the limitations placed on one's free development with a duller self-protecting sensibility without which it would be difficult to function in a society like our own.

The revelation of the deceptive character of social reality brings with it another transformation in the way the social milieu is present in feminist experience. Just as so many apparently innocent things are really devices to enforce compliance, so are many "ordinary" sorts of situations transformed into opportunities or occasions for struggle against the system. In a light-hearted mood, I embark upon a Christmas shopping expedition, only to have it turn, as if independent of my will, into an occasion for striking a blow against sexism. On holiday from political struggle and even political principle, I have abandoned myself to the richly sensuous albeit repellantly bourgeois atmosphere of Marshall Field's. I wander about the toy department, looking at chemistry sets and miniature ironing boards. Then, unbidden, the following thought flashes into my head: What if, just this once, I send a doll to my nephew and an erector set to my niece? Will this confirm the growing suspicion in my family that I am a crank? What if the children themselves misunderstand my gesture and covet one another's gifts? Worse, what if the boy believes that I have somehow insulted him? The shopping trip turned occasion for resistance now becomes a *test*. I will have to answer for this, once it becomes clear that Marshall Field's has not unwittingly switched the labels. My husband will be embarrassed. A didactic role will be thrust upon me, even though I had determined earlier that the situation was not ripe for consciousness-raising. The special ridicule which is reserved for feminists will be heaped upon me at the next family party, all in good fun, of course.

Whether she lives a fairly conventional life or an unconventional one, ordinary social life presents to the feminist an unending sequence of such occasions and each occasion is a test. It is not easy to live under the strain of constant testing. Some tests we pass with honor, but often as not we fail, and the price of failure is self-reproach and the shame of having copped out. To further complicate things, much of the time it is not clear what criteria would allow us to distinguish the honorable outcome of an occasion from a dishonorable one. Must I seize every opportunity? May I never take the easy way out? Is what I call prudence and good sense merely cowardice? On the occasion in question I compromised and sent both children musical instruments.

The transformation of day-to-day living into a series of invitations to struggle has the important consequence for the feminist that she finds herself, for a while at least, in an ethical and existential impasse. She no longer knows what sort of person she ought to be and, therefore, she does not know what she ought to do. One moral paradigm is called into question by the partial and laborious emergence of another. The ethical issues involved in the occasion of my shopping trip were relatively trivial, but this is not true of all occasions. One thinks of Nora's decision in *A Doll's House* to leave her husband and children and seek independence and self-fulfillment on her own. The case is an extreme one, but it illustrates what I have in mind. Here, the conflict is between one moral commitment and another, between, on the one hand, a Nietzschean transvaluation of received values for the sake of a heroic and creative self-surpassing and, on the other, a Christian ideal of devotion to others, self-abnegation, and self-sacrifice. But Nora makes the decision too easily. Ibsen, her creator, betrays a certain lack of sensitivity to feminist experience: A real-life Nora would have suffered more.

To whom will a woman in such a predicament turn for guidance? To choose a moral authority, as Sartre tells us, is already to anticipate what kind of advice we are prepared to take seriously. Having become aware of the self-serving way in which a male-dominated culture has defined goodness for the female, she may decide on principle that the person she wants to be will have little in her character of patience, meekness, complaisance, self-sacrifice, or any of the other "feminine" virtues. But will such a solution satisfy a reflective person? Must the duty I have to myself (if we have duties to ourselves) *always* win out over the duty I have to others? Even an unreflective person, who might not ask such questions, cannot fail to see that the way out of her dilemma may cause great suffering to the people closest to her. To develop feminist consciousness is to live a part of one's life in the sort of *ambiguous ethical situation* which existentialist writers have been most adept at describing. Here it might be objected that the feature of feminist experience I have been describing is characteristic not of a fully emergent feminist consciousness but of periods of transition to such consciousness, that the feminist is a person who has chosen her moral paradigm and who no longer suffers the inner conflicts of those in ambiguous moral predicaments. I would deny this. Even the woman who has decided to be this new person and not that old one, can be tormented by recurring doubts. Moreover, the pain inflicted in the course of finding one's way out of an existential impasse, one continues to inflict. One thing, however, is clear: The feminist is someone who, at the very least, has been marked by the experience of ethical ambiguity; she is a moral agent with a distinctive history.

Feminist consciousness, it was suggested earlier, can be understood as the negating and transcending awareness of one's own relationship to a society heavy with the weight of its own contradictions. The inner conflicts and divisions which make up so much of this experience are just the ways in which each of us, in the uniqueness of her own situation and personality, lives these contradictions. In sum, feminist consciousness is the consciousness of a being radically alienated from her world and often divided against herself, a being who sees herself as victim and whose victimization determines her being-in-the-world as resistance, wariness, and suspicion. Raw and exposed much of the time, she suffers from both ethical and ontological shock. Lacking a fully formed moral paradigm, sometimes unable to make sense of her own reactions and emotions, she is immersed in a social reality which exhibits to her an aspect of malevolent ambiguity. Many "ordinary" social situations and many human encounters organized for quite a different end she apprehends as occasions for struggle, as frequently exhausting tests of her will and resolve. She is an outsider to her society, to many of the people she loves, and to the still unemancipated elements in her own personality.

This picture is not as bleak as it appears; indeed, its "bleakness" would be seen in proper perspective had I described what things were like *before*. Coming to have a feminist consciousness is the experience of coming to see things about oneself and one's society that were heretofore hidden. This experience, the acquiring of a "raised" consciousness, in spite of its disturbing aspects, is an immeasurable advance over that false consciousness which it replaces. The scales fall from our eyes. We are no longer required to struggle against unreal enemies, to put others' interests ahead of our own, or to hate ourselves. We begin to understand why we have such depreciated images of ourselves and why so many of us are lacking any genuine conviction of personal worth. Understanding, even beginning to understand this, makes it possible to *change*. Coming to see things differently, we are able to make out possibilities for liberating collective action and for unprecedented personal growth, possibilities which a deceptive sexist social reality had heretofore concealed. No longer do we have to practice upon ourselves that mutilation of intellect and personality required of individuals who, caught up in an irrational and destructive system, are nevertheless not allowed to regard it as anything but sane, progressive, and normal. Moreover, that feeling of alienation from established society which is so prominent a feature of feminist experience may be counterbalanced by a new identification with women of all conditions and a growing sense of solidarity with other feminists. It is a fitting commentary on our society that the growth of feminist consciousness, in spite of its ambiguities, confusions, and trials, is apprehended by those in whom it develops as an experience of liberation.

2

On Psychological Oppression

In *Black Skin, White Masks,* Frantz Fanon offers an anguished and eloquent description of the psychological effects of colonialism on the colonized, a "clinical study" of what he calls the "psychic alienation of the black man." "Those who recognize themselves in it," he says, "will have made a step forward."[1] Fanon's black American readers saw at once that he had captured the corrosive effects not only of classic colonial oppression but of domestic racism too, and that his study fitted well the picture of black America as an internal colony. Without wanting in any way to diminish the oppressive and stifling realities of black experience that Fanon reveals, let me say that I, a white woman, recognize myself in this book too, not only in my "shameful livery of white incomprehension,"[2] but as myself the victim of a "psychic alienation" similar to the one Fanon has described. In this paper I shall try to explore that moment of recognition, to reveal the ways in which the psychological effects of sexist oppression resemble those of racism and colonialism.

To oppress, says Webster, is "to lie heavy on, to weigh down, to exercise harsh dominion over." When we describe a people as oppressed, what we have in mind most often is an oppression that is economic and political in character. But recent liberation movements, the black liberation movement and the women's movement in particular, have brought to light forms of oppression that are not immediately economic or political. It is possible to be oppressed in ways that need involve neither physical deprivation, legal inequality, nor economic exploitation;[3] one can be oppressed psychologically—the "psychic alienation" of which Fanon speaks. To be psychologically oppressed is to be weighed down in your mind; it is to have a harsh dominion exercised over your self-esteem. The psychologically oppressed become their own oppressors; they come to exercise harsh dominion over their own self-esteem. Differently put, psychological oppression can be regarded as the "internalization of intimations of inferiority."[4]

Like economic oppression, psychological oppression is institutionalized and systematic; it serves to make the work of domination easier by breaking the spirit of the dominated and by rendering them incapable of understanding the nature of those agencies responsible for their subjugation. This allows those who benefit from the established order of things to maintain their ascendancy with more appearance of legitimacy and with less recourse to overt acts of violence than they might otherwise require. Now, poverty and powerlessness can destroy a person's self-esteem, and the fact that one occupies an inferior position in society is all too often racked up to one's being an inferior sort of person. Clearly, then, economic and political oppression are themselves psychologically oppressive. But there are unique modes of psychological oppression that can be distinguished from the usual forms of economic and political domination. Fanon offers a series of what are essentially phenomenological descriptions of psychic alienation.[5] In spite of considerable overlapping, the experiences of oppression he describes fall into three categories: stereotyping, cultural domination, and sexual objectification. These, I shall contend, are some of the ways in which the terrible messages of inferiority can be delivered even to those who may enjoy certain material benefits; they are special modes of psychic alienation. In what follows, I shall examine some of the ways in which American women—white women and women of color—are stereotyped, culturally dominated, and sexually objectified. In the course of the discussion, I shall argue that our ordinary concept of oppression needs to be altered and expanded, for it is too restricted to encompass what an analysis of psychological oppression reveals about the nature of oppression in general. Finally, I shall be concerned throughout to show how both fragmentation and mystification are present in each mode of psychological oppression, although in varying degrees: fragmentation, the splitting of the whole person into parts of a person which, in stereotyping, may take the form of a war between a "true" and "false" self—or, in sexual objectification, the form of an often coerced and degrading identification of a person with her body; mystification, the systematic obscuring of both the reality and agencies of psychological oppression so that its intended effect, the depreciated self, is lived out as destiny, guilt, or neurosis.

The stereotypes that sustain sexism are similar in many ways to those that sustain racism. Like white women, black and brown persons of both sexes have been regarded as childlike, happiest when they are occupying their "place"; more intuitive than rational, more spontaneous than deliberate, closer to nature, and less capable of substantial cultural accomplishment. Black men and women of all races have been victims of sexual stereotyping: the black man and the black woman, like the "Latin spitfire," are lustful and hotblooded; they are thought to lack the capacities for instinctual control that distinguish people from animals. What is seen as an excess in persons of color appears as a deficiency in the white woman; comparatively frigid, she has been, nonetheless, defined by her sexuality as well, here her reproductive role or function. In regard to capability and competence, black women have, again, an excess of what in white women is a deficiency. White women have been seen as incapable and incompetent: no matter, for these are traits of the truly feminine woman. Black women, on the other hand, have been seen as overly capable, hence, as unfeminine bitches who threaten, through their very competence, to castrate their men.

Stereotyping is morally reprehensible as well as psychologically oppressive on two counts, at least. First, it can hardly be expected that those who hold a set of stereotyped beliefs about the sort of person I am will understand my needs or even respect my rights. Second, suppose that I, the object of some stereotype, believe in it myself—for why should I not believe what everyone else believes? I may then find it difficult to achieve what existentialists call an authentic choice of self, or what some psychologists have regarded as a state of self-actualization. Moral philosophers have quite correctly placed a high value, sometimes the highest value, on the development of autonomy and moral agency. Clearly, the economic and political domination of women—our concrete powerlessness—is what threatens our autonomy most. But stereotyping, in its own way, threatens our self-determination too. Even when economic and political obstacles on the path to autonomy are removed, a depreciated alter ego still blocks the way. It is hard enough for me to determine what sort of person I am or ought to try to become without being shadowed by an alternate self, a truncated and inferior self that I have, in some sense, been doomed to be all the time. For many, the prefabricated self triumphs over a more authentic self which, with work and encouragement, might sometime have emerged. For the talented few, retreat into the *imago* is raised to the status of art or comedy. Muhammad Ali has made himself what he could scarcely escape being made into—a personification of Primitive Man; while Zsa Zsa Gabor is not so much a woman as the parody of a woman.

Female stereotypes threaten the autonomy of women not only by virtue of their existence but also by virtue of their content.[6] In the conventional portrait, women deny their femininity when they undertake action that is too self-regarding or independent. As we have seen, black women are condemned (often by black men) for supposedly having done this already; white women stand under an injunction not to follow their example. Many women in many places lacked (and many still lack) the elementary right to choose our own mates; but for some women even in our own society today, this is virtually the only major decision we are thought capable of making without putting our womanly nature in danger; what follows ever after is or ought to be a properly feminine submission to the decisions of men. We cannot be autonomous, as men are thought to be autonomous, without in some sense ceasing to be women. When one considers how interwoven are traditional female stereotypes with traditional female roles—and these, in turn, with the ways in which we are socialized—all this is seen in an even more sinister light: White women, at least, are psychologically conditioned not to pursue the kind of autonomous development that is held by the culture to be a constitutive feature of masculinity.

The truncated self I am to be is not something manufactured out there by an anonymous Other which I encounter only in the pages of *Playboy* or the *Ladies' Home Journal;* it is inside of me, a part of myself. I may become infatuated with my feminine persona and waste my powers in the more or less hopeless pursuit of a *Vogue* figure, the look of an *Essence* model, or a home that "expresses my personality." Or I may find the parts of myself fragmented and the fragments at war with one another. Women are only now learning to identify and struggle against the forces that have laid these psychic burdens upon us. More often than not, we live out this struggle, which is really a struggle against oppression, in a mystified way: What we are enduring we believe to be entirely intrapsychic in character, the result of immaturity, maladjustment, or even neurosis.

Tyler, the great classical anthropologist, defined culture as all the items in the general life of a people. To claim that women are victims of cultural domination is to claim that all the items in the general life of our people—our language, our institutions, our art and literature, our popular culture—are sexist; that all, to a greater or lesser degree, manifest male supremacy. There is some exaggeration in this claim, but not much. Unlike the black colonial whom Fanon describes with such pathos, women *qua* women are not now in possession of an alternate culture, a "native" culture which, even if regarded by everyone, including ourselves, as decidedly inferior to the dominant culture, we could at least recognize as our own. However degraded or distorted an image of ourselves we see reflected in the patriarchal culture, the culture of our men is still our culture. Certainly in some respects, the condition of women is like the condition of a colonized people. But we are not a colonized people; we have never been more than half a people.[7]

This lack of cultural autonomy has several important consequences for an understanding of the condition of women. A culture has a global character; hence, the limits of my culture are the limits of my world. The subordination of women, then, because it is so pervasive a feature of my culture, will (if uncontested) appear to be natural—and because it is natural, unalterable. Unlike a colonized people, women have no memory of a "time before": a time before the masters came, a time before we were subjugated and ruled. Further, since one function of cultural identity is to allow me to distinguish those who are like me from those who are not, I may feel more kinship with those who share my culture, even though they oppress me, than with the women of another culture, whose whole experience of life may well be closer to my own than to any man's.

Our true situation in regard to male supremacist culture is one of domination and exclusion. But this manifests itself in an extremely deceptive way; mystification once more holds sway. Our relative absence from the "higher" culture is taken as proof that we are unable to participate in it ("Why are there no great women artists?"). Theories of the female nature must then be brought forward to try to account for this.[8] The splitting or fragmenting of women's consciousness which takes place in the cultural sphere is also apparent. While remaining myself, I must at the same time transform myself into that abstract and "universal" subject for whom cultural artifacts are made and whose values and experience they express. This subject is not universal at all, however, but *male.* Thus, I must approve the taming of the shrew, laugh at the mother-in-law or the dumb blonde, and somehow identify with all those heroes of fiction from Faust to the personae of Norman Mailer and Henry Miller, whose *Bildungsgeschichten* involve the sexual exploitation of women. Women of color have, of course, a special problem: The dominant cultural subject is not only male, but *white,* so their cultural alienation is doubled; they are expected to assimilate cultural motifs that are not only masculinist but racist.[9]

Women of all races and ethnicities, like Fanon's "black man," are subject not only to stereotyping and cultural depreciation but to sexual objectification as well. Even though much has been written about sexual objectification in the literature of the women's movement, the notion itself is complex, obscure, and much in need of philosophical clarification. I offer the following preliminary characterization of sexual objectification: A person is sexually objectified when her sexual parts or sexual functions are separated out from the rest of her personality and reduced to the status of mere instruments or else regarded as if they were capable of representing her. On this definition, then, the prostitute would be a victim of sexual objectification, as would the *Playboy* bunny, the female breeder, and the bathing beauty.

To say that the sexual part of a person is regarded as if it could represent her is to imply that it cannot, that the part and the whole are incommensurable. But surely there are times, in the sexual embrace perhaps, when a woman might want to be regarded as nothing but a sexually intoxicating body and when attention paid to some other aspect of her person—say, to her mathematical ability—would be absurdly out of place. If sexual relations involve some sexual objectification, then it becomes necessary to distinguish situations in which sexual objectification is oppressive from the sorts of situations in which it is not.[10] The identification of a person with her sexuality becomes oppressive, one might venture, when such an identification becomes habitually extended into every area of her experience. To be routinely perceived by others in a sexual light on occasions when such a perception is inappropriate is to have one's very being subjected to that compulsive sexualization that has been the traditional lot of both white women and black men and women of color generally. "For the majority of white men," says Fanon, "the Negro is the incarnation of a genital potency beyond all moralities and prohibitions."[11] Later in *Black Skin, White Masks,* he writes that "the Negro is the genital."[12]

One way to be sexually objectified, then, is to be the object of a kind of perception, unwelcome and inappropriate, that takes the part for the whole. An example may make this clearer. A young woman was recently interviewed for a teaching job in philosophy by the academic chairman of a large department. During most of the interview, so she reported, the man stared fixedly at her breasts. In this situation, the woman is a bosom, not a job candidate. Was this department chairman guilty only of a confusion between business and pleasure? Scarcely. He stares at her breasts for his sake, not hers. Her wants and needs not only play no role in the encounter but, because of the direction of his attention, she is discomfited, feels humiliated, and performs badly. Not surprisingly, she fails to get the job. Much of the time, sexual objectification occurs independently of what women want; it is something done to us against our will. It is clear from this example that the objectifying perception that splits a person into parts serves to elevate one interest above another. Now it stands revealed not only as a way of perceiving, but as a way of maintaining dominance as well. It is not clear to me that the sexual and nonsexual spheres of experience can or ought to be kept separate forever (Marcuse, for one, has envisioned the eroticization of all areas of human life); but as things stand now, sexualization is one way of fixing disadvantaged persons in their disadvantage, to their clear detriment and within a narrow and repressive eros.

Consider now a second example of the way in which that fragmenting perception, which is so large an ingredient in the sexual objectification of women, serves to maintain the dominance of men. It is a fine spring day, and with an utter lack of self-consciousness, I am bouncing down the street. Suddenly I hear men's voices. Catcalls and whistles fill the air. These noises are clearly sexual in intent and they are meant for me; they come from across the street. I freeze. As Sartre would say, I have been petrified by the gaze of the Other. My face flushes and my motions become stiff and self-conscious. The body which only a moment before I inhabited with such ease now floods my consciousness. I have been made into an object. While it is true that for these men I am nothing but, let us say, a "nice piece of ass," there is more involved in this encounter than their mere fragmented perception of me. They could, after all, have enjoyed me in silence. Blissfully unaware, breasts bouncing, eyes on the birds in the trees, I could have passed by without having been turned to stone. But I must be *made* to know that I am a "nice piece of ass": I must be made to see myself as they see me. There is an element of compulsion in this encounter, in this being-made-to-be-aware of one's own flesh; like being made to apologize, it is humiliating. It is unclear what role is played by sexual arousal or even sexual connoisseurship in encounters like these. What I describe seems less the spontaneous expression of a healthy eroticism than a ritual of subjugation.

Sexual objectification as I have characterized it involves two persons: the one who objectifies and the one who is objectified. But the observer and the one observed can be the same person. I can, of course, take pleasure in my own body as another might take pleasure in it and it would be naive not to notice that there are delights of a narcissistic kind that go along with the status ''sex object.'' But the extent to which the identification of women with their bodies feeds an essentially infantile narcissism—an attitude of mind in keeping with our forced infantilization in other areas of life—is, at least for me, an open question. Subject to the evaluating eye of the male connoisseur, women learn to evaluate themselves first and best. Our identities can no more be kept separate from the appearance of our bodies than they can be kept separate from the shadow-selves of the female stereotype. ''Much of a young woman's identity is already defined in her kind of attractiveness and in the selectivity of her search for the man (or men) by whom she wishes to be sought.''[13] There is something obsessional in the preoccupation of many women with their bodies, although the magnitude of the obsession will vary somewhat with the presence or absence in a woman's life of other sources of self-esteem and with her capacity to gain a living independent of her looks. Surrounded on all sides by images of perfect female beauty—for, in modern advertising, the needs of capitalism and the traditional values of patriarchy are happily married—of course we fall short. The narcissism encouraged by our identification with the body is shattered by these images. Whose nose is not the wrong shape, whose hips are not too wide or too narrow? Anyone who believes that such concerns are too trivial to weigh very heavily with most women has failed to grasp the realities of the feminine condition.

The idea that women ought always to make themselves as pleasing to the eye as possible is very widespread indeed. It was dismaying to come across this passage in a paper written by an eminent Marxist humanist in defense of the contemporary women's movement:

> There is no reason why a woman's liberation activist should not try to look pretty and attractive. One of the universal human aspirations of all times was to raise reality to the level of art, to make the world more beautiful, to be more beautiful within given limits. Beauty is a value in itself; it will always be respected and will attract—to be sure various forms of beauty but not to the exclusion of physical beauty. A woman does not become a sex object in herself, or only because of her pretty appearance. She becomes a sexual object in relationship, when she allows a man to treat her in a certain depersonalizing, degrading way; and vice versa, a woman does not become a sexual subject by neglecting her appearance.[14]

It is not for the sake of mere men that we women—not just we women, but we women's liberation activists—ought to look ''pretty and attractive,'' but for the sake of something much more exalted: for the sake of beauty. This preoccupation with the way we look and the fear that women might stop trying to make themselves pretty and attractive (so as to ''raise reality to the level of art'') would be a species of objectification anywhere; but it is absurdly out of place in a paper on women's emancipation. It is as if an essay on the black liberation movement were to end by admonishing blacks not to forget their natural rhythm, or as if Marx had warned the workers of the world not to neglect their appearance while throwing off their chains.

Markovic's concern with women's appearance merely reflects a larger cultural preoccupation. It is a fact that women in our society are regarded as having a virtual duty "to make the most of what we have." But the imperative not to neglect our appearance suggests that we can neglect it, that it is within our power to make ourselves look better—not just neater and cleaner, but prettier, and more attractive. What is presupposed by this is that we don't look good enough already, that attention to the ordinary standards of hygiene would be insufficient, that there is something wrong with us as we are. Here, the "intimations of inferiority" are clear: Not only must we continue to produce ourselves as beautiful bodies, but the bodies we have to work with are deficient to begin with. Even within an already inferiorized identity (i.e., the identity of one who is principally and most importantly a body), I turn out once more to be inferior, for the body I am to be, never sufficient unto itself, stands forever in need of plucking or painting, of slimming down or fattening up, of firming or flattening.

The foregoing examination of three modes of psychological oppression, so it appears, points up the need for an alteration in our ordinary concept of oppression. Oppression, I believe, is ordinarily conceived in too limited a fashion. This has placed undue restrictions both on our understanding of what oppression itself is and on the categories of persons we might want to classify as oppressed. Consider, for example, the following paradigmatic case of oppression:

> And the Egyptians made the children of Israel to serve with rigor; and they made their lives bitter with hard bondage, in mortar and in brick, and in all manner of service in the field; all their service wherein they made them serve, was with rigor.[15]

Here the Egyptians, one group of persons, exercise harsh dominion over the Israelites, another group of persons. It is not suggested that the Israelites, however great their sufferings, have lost their integrity and wholeness *qua* persons. But psychological oppression is dehumanizing and depersonalizing; it attacks the person in her personhood. I mean by this that the nature of psychological oppression is such that the oppressor and oppressed alike come to doubt that the oppressed have the capacity to do the sorts of things that only persons can do, to be what persons, in the fullest sense of the term, can be. The possession of autonomy, for example, is widely thought to distinguish persons from nonpersons; but some female stereotypes, as we have seen, threaten the autonomy of women. Oppressed people might or might not be in a position to exercise their autonomy, but the psychologically oppressed may come to believe that they lack the capacity to be autonomous whatever their position.

Similarly, the creation of culture is a distinctly human function, perhaps the most human function. In its cultural life, a group is able to affirm its values and to grasp its identity in acts of self-reflection. Frequently, oppressed persons, cut off from the cultural apparatus, are denied the exercise of this function entirely. To the extent that we are able to catch sight of ourselves in the dominant culture at all, the images we see are distorted or demeaning. Finally, sexual objectification leads to the identification of those who undergo it with what is both human and not quite human—the body. Thus, psychological oppression is just what Fanon said it was—"psychic alienation"—the estrangement or separating of a person from some of the essential attributes of personhood.

Mystification surrounds these processes of human estrangement. The special modes of psychological oppression can be regarded as some of the many ways in which messages of inferiority are delivered to those who are to occupy an inferior position in society. But it is important to remember that messages of this sort are neither sent nor received in an unambiguous way. We are taught that white women and (among others) black men and women are deficient in those capacities that distinguish persons from nonpersons, but at the same time we are assured that we are persons after all. *Of course* women are persons; *of course* blacks are human beings. Who but the lunatic fringe would deny it? The Antillean Negro, Fanon is fond of repeating, is a *Frenchman*. The official ideology announces with conviction that "all men are created equal"; and in spite of the suspect way in which this otherwise noble assertion is phrased, we women learn that they mean to include us after all.

It is itself psychologically oppressive both to believe and at the same time not to believe that one is inferior—in other words, to believe a contradiction. Lacking an analysis of the larger system of social relations which produced it, one can only make sense of this contradiction in two ways. First, while accepting in some quite formal sense the proposition that "all men are created equal," I can believe, inconsistently, what my oppressors have always believed: that some types of persons are less equal than others. I may then live out my membership in my sex or race in *shame;* I am "only a woman" or "just a nigger." Or, somewhat more consistently, I may reject entirely the belief that my disadvantage is generic; but having still to account for it somehow, I may locate the cause squarely within myself, a bad destiny of an entirely private sort—a character flaw, an "inferiority complex," or a neurosis.

Many oppressed persons come to regard themselves as uniquely unable to satisfy normal criteria of psychological health or moral adequacy. To believe that my inferiority is a function of the kind of person I am may make me ashamed of being one of *this* kind. On the other hand, a lack I share with many others just because of an accident of birth would be unfortunate indeed, but at least I would not have to regard myself as having failed uniquely to measure up to standards that people like myself are expected to meet. It should be pointed out, however, that both of these "resolutions"—the ascription of one's inferiority to idiosyncratic or else to generic causes—produces a "poor self-image," a bloodless term of the behavioral sciences that refers to a very wide variety of possible ways to suffer.[16]

To take one's oppression to be an inherent flaw of birth, or of psychology, is to have what Marxists have characterized as "false consciousness." Systematically deceived as we are about the nature and origin of our unhappiness, our struggles are directed inward toward the self, or toward other similar selves in whom we may see our deficiencies mirrored, not outward upon those social forces responsible for our predicament. Like the psychologically disturbed, the psychologically oppressed often lack a viable identity. Frequently we are unable to make sense of our own impulses or feelings, not only because our drama of fragmentation gets played out on an inner psychic stage, but because we are forced to find our way about in a world which presents itself to us in a masked and deceptive fashion. Regarded as persons, yet depersonalized, we are treated by our society the way the parents of some schizophrenics are said by R. D. Laing to treat their children—professing love at the very moment they shrink from their children's touch.

In sum, then, to be psychologically oppressed is to be caught in the double bind of a society which both affirms my human status and at the same time bars me from the exercise of many of those typically human functions that bestow this status. To be denied an autonomous choice of self, forbidden cultural expression, and condemned to the immanence of mere bodily being is to be cut off from the sorts of activities that define what it is to be human. A person whose being has been subjected to these cleavages may be described as "alienated." Alienation in any form causes a rupture within the human person, an estrangement from self, a "splintering of human nature into a number of misbegotten parts."[17] Any adequate theory of the nature and varieties of human alienation, then, must encompass psychological oppression—or, to use Fanon's term once more, "psychic alienation."

Much has been written about alienation, but it is Marx's theory of alienation that speaks most compellingly to the concerns of feminist political theory. Alienation for Marx is primarily the alienation of labor. What distinguishes human beings from animals is "labor"—for Marx, the free, conscious, and creative transformation of nature in accordance with human needs. But under capitalism, workers are alienated in production, estranged from the products of their labor, from their own productive activity, and from their fellow workers.

Human productive activity, according to Marx, is "objectified" in its products. What this means is that we are able to grasp ourselves reflectively primarily in the things we have produced; human needs and powers become concrete "in their products as the amount and type of change which their exercise has brought about."[18] But in capitalist production, the capitalist has a right to appropriate what workers have produced. Thus, the product goes to augment capital, where it becomes part of an alien force exercising power over those who produced it. An "objectification" or extension of the worker's self, the product is split off from this self and turned against it. But workers are alienated not only from the products they produce but from their own laboring activity as well, for labor under capitalism is not, as labor should be, an occasion for human self-realization but mere drudgery which "mortifies the body and ruins the mind."[19] The worker's labor "is therefore not voluntary, but coerced; it is forced labor. It is therefore not the satisfaction of a need; it is merely a means to satisfy needs external to it."[20] When the free and creative productive activity that should define human functioning is reduced to a mere means to sustain life, to "forced labor," workers suffer fragmentation and loss of self. Since labor is the most characteristic human life activity, to be alienated from one's own labor is to be estranged from oneself.

In many ways, psychic alienation and the alienation of labor are profoundly alike. Both involve a splitting off of human functions from the human person, a forbidding of activities thought to be essential to a fully human existence. Both subject the individual to fragmentation and impoverishment. Alienation is not a condition into which someone might stumble by accident; it has come both to the victim of psychological oppression and to the alienated worker from without, as a usurpation by someone else of what is, by rights, *not his to usurp.*[21] Alienation occurs in each case when activities which not only belong to the domain of the self but define, in large measure, the proper functioning of this self, fall under the control of others. To be a victim of alienation is to have a part of one's being stolen by another. Both psychic alienation and the alienation of labor might be regarded as varieties of alienated productivity. From this perspective, cultural domination would be the estrangement or alienation of production in the cultural sphere; while the subjective effects of stereotyping as well as the self-objectification that regularly accompanies sexual objectification could be interpreted as an alienation in the production of one's own person.

All the modes of oppression—psychological, political, and economic—and the kinds of alienation they generate serve to maintain a vast system of privilege—privilege of race, of sex, and of class. Every mode of oppression within the system has its own part to play, but each serves to support and to maintain the others. Thus, for example, the assault on the self-esteem of white women and of black persons of both sexes prepares us for the historic role that a disproportionate number of us are destined to play within the process of production: that of a cheap or reserve labor supply. Class oppression, in turn, encourages those who are somewhat higher in the hierarchies of race or gender to cling to a false sense of superiority—a poor compensation indeed. Because of the interlocking character of the modes of oppression, I think it highly unlikely that any form of oppression will disappear entirely until the system of oppression as a whole is overthrown.

3

Narcissism, Femininity, and Alienation

One of the many things men don't understand about women is the extent
to which our self-esteem depends on how we feel we look at any given
moment—and how much we yearn for a compliment, at any age. If I had
just won the Nobel Peace Prize but felt my hair looked awful, I would not
be glowing with self-assurance when I entered the room.

—Dinah Shore[1]

"Femininity" as Alienation

An important new body of theory is being born out of what Amy Bridges
and Heidi Hartmann have called "the Unhappy Marriage of Marxism and Feminism."[2] The name most commonly given to the offspring of this union is "socialist feminism," even though many of those who are most responsible for its
emergence are not agreed on what to call it.[3] Tentative, impressionistic, and
clearly unfinished, socialist feminism has nevertheless identified and in many
cases transcended the limitations of both bourgeois feminism and orthodox
Marxism. Socialist feminists have dealt the traditional Marxist account of the
origins of partriarchy a blow from which it is unlikely ever to recover.[4] They
have exposed the fatal lack in traditional Marxism both of a theory of sexuality
and of an adequate account of human psychological development, and have
begun to formulate theory in these areas from a historical materialist perspective
with challenging results.[5] Further, socialist feminists have subjected several of
the central categories of Marxist analysis to searching critical scrutiny, chiefly
the categories of "production" and of "relations of production." They have
claimed that these categories are conceived too narrowly to allow an adequate
understanding either of the oppressive character of the relations between men
and women or of what in fact constitutes the proper economic or productive
"base" of society.[6]

One of the tasks which socialist feminists have yet to accomplish is the
alteration and elaboration of Marx's theory of alienation. Marx's account of the
alienation of labor is both normative and descriptive: It is at once a powerful
indictment of the capitalist system and an accurate description of some of the
more salient features of that system. According to Marx, the alienated or estranged worker is self-estranged, not in the sense that the self is the agent of
its own alienation (though Marx sometimes seems to suggest this), but because

the state of alienation consists in the prohibition of those activities which are constitutive of selfhood. For Marx, labor is the most distinctively human activity; following Hegel, he regards the product of labor as an exteriorization of the worker's being, an objectification of human powers and abilities. But under capitalism, workers are alienated from the products of their labor as well as from their own productive activity. The capitalist organization of production is such that workers lose control of what they have produced; their products cease to be mirrors in which they are able both to affirm and to enlarge their distinctively human capacities; these products serve instead to enrich the capitalist and to augment the power of capital, an "alien force" inimical to the worker's vital interests. The loss of the product has its analogue in the worker's loss of control over his or her own productive activity. What distinguishes human "species being" from the being of other species is our distinctive laboring activity: This Marx regards as the free, self-aware, and creative transformation of nature in accord with human needs. But under capitalism, work is degraded. Most workers lack any opportunity for artistic or intellectual development; far from allowing workers to affirm or to augment their essential human powers, work under capitalism is forced labor to which the worker goes each day like a prisoner condemned, a mere drudgery which "mortifies the body and ruins the mind."[7]

The concept of alienation employed by Marx has two core features: It refers both to a *fragmentation* of the human person and to a *prohibition* on the exercise of typically human functions.[8] When workers lose control of the products of their labor or of their own productive activity, they have undergone fragmentation within their own persons, a kind of inner impoverishment; parts of their being have fallen under the control of another. This fragmentation is the consequence of a form of social organization which has given to some persons the power to prohibit other persons from the full exercise of capacities the exercise of which is thought necessary to a fully human existence.

If we understand alienation in this way, it can be seen that Marx's theory of alienation, focused as it is on that fragmentation of the self which is a consequence of the organization of material production under capitalism, may well apply to women insofar as we are workers, but not insofar as we are women. Women undergo a special sort of fragmentation and loss of being *as* women: Women suffer modes of alienation which are absent from Marx's account and which can be distinguished from the ways in which all workers, men and women alike, are alienated under the prevailing system of material production.

From this perspective, then, we may regard many parts of the emerging feminist critique of patriarchy as building blocks of a new theory of alienation, a refined and comprehensive theory able to incorporate Marx's insights into the nature of the human condition under capitalism and at the same time to grasp what is specific to the experience of women in a way that orthodox Marxism has failed to do. Some examples of distinctively feminine modes of alienation may make this clearer. The cultural domination of women, for example, may be regarded as a species of alienation, for women as women are clearly alienated in cultural production. Most avenues of cultural expression—high culture, popular culture, even to some extent language—are instruments of male supremacy. Women have little control over the cultural apparatus itself and are often entirely absent from its products; to the extent that we are not excluded from it entirely, the images of ourselves we see reflected in the dominant culture are often truncated or demeaning. Human beings begin to distinguish themselves from animals not only, as Marx says, when they start to produce their own means of subsistence, but when they begin to invent modes of cultural expression, such as myth, ritual, and art, which make possible the bestowal of meaning upon their own activity. If this is so, then the prohibition on cultural expression denies to women the right to develop and to exercise capacities which define, in part, what it means to be human.

The historic suppression and distortion of the erotic requirements of women are clearly an instance of *sexual* alienation, for just as workers can be alienated from their labor, so can women be estranged from their own sexuality. The double standard of sexual morality, still widely in force, is pertinent here, as are the now discredited but formerly influential theories of innate female sexual passivity and of the dual orgasm. Sexual alienation itself is only one manifestation of a larger alienation from the body. Iris Young has described the ways in which

> the norms of femininity suppress the body potential of women. We grow up learning that the feminine body is soft, not muscular, passive, incapable, vulnerable. Our parents, teachers and friends suppress our natural urges to run, jump, risk, by cries that we should not act so boldly and move so daringly . . . . Developing a sense of our bodies as beautiful objects to be gazed at and decorated requires suppressing a sense of our bodies as strong, active subjects moving out to meet the world's risks and confront the resistances of matter and motion.[9]

Young also argues that restrictions on feminine body comportment generate a restricted spatiality in women as well, a sense that the body is positioned within invisible spatial barriers.

If women are alienated from the body in these ways, we suffer a different form of estrangement by being too closely identified with it in others. Sexual objectification occurs when a woman's sexual parts or sexual functions are separated out from her person, reduced to the status of mere instruments, or else regarded as if they were capable of representing her.[10] To be dealt with in this way is to have one's entire being identified with the body, a thing which in many religious and metaphysical systems, as well as in the popular mind, has been regarded as less intrinsically valuable, indeed, as less inherently human, than the mind or personality. Clearly, sexual objectification is a form of fragmentation and thus an impoverishment of the objectified individual; it involves too the implicit denial to those who suffer it that they have capacities which transcend the merely sexual.

A socialist feminist theory of the alienation of women has yet to take precise theoretical shape. All the modes of such alienation will have to be uncovered and examined both in their relationships to one another and to the modes of estrangement described by Marx. The agents and occasions of such alienation will have to be identified. The estrangements attendant not only upon class and sex but upon race as well will have to be integrated into such a theory. That structuring of the unconscious both in men and women which facilitates the reproduction of alienated modes of existence will have to be revealed.

The development of such a theory, so it seems, is an urgent and compelling task for feminist political thought. But there is one salient difference between the alienation of labor and the notion of femininity as alienation, a difference which may threaten to sabotage the project at the start. It would be odd to regard something as alienating if it were not, by and large, disagreeable. Workers may have to engage in alienated labor because they lack any other way of making a living, but they do not go enthusiastically to the assembly line. Worker dissatisfaction, as everyone knows, has been amply documented, by Marxist and non-Marxist social scientists alike. But however unwilling feminists may be to admit it, many women appear to embrace with enthusiasm what seem to be the most alienated aspects of feminine existence. There is no dearth of candidates for Playmate of the Month. Most teenage girls would rather be Miss America than Madame Curie. Thousands of women have been attracted to movements like "Fascinating Womanhood" which aim both to safeguard and to promote the more objectionable norms of femininity. Women of all classes buy large numbers of books and magazines which teach them how to be better, i.e., more "feminine," women. There is no comparable body of popular literature which teaches workers to be better workers: In fact, that sort of training is generally imposed on people against their will, first in school, later by the boss or foreman. Workers resist alienated labor, if not militantly, then at the very least in small acts of sabotage or in fantasy.

We must determine whether the gratifications of "womanliness" do indeed constitute counterexamples to the claim that much of what is held out to us as "femininity" is in fact alienation. Since it will be impossible here to examine or even to identify everything that might qualify as a pleasure of this sort, I have selected a paradigm case, the case of so-called feminine narcissism. Sexual objectification, I argued earlier, displays the characteristic marks of alienation. Now, sexual objectification typically involves two persons, one who objectifies and one who is objectified. But objectifier and objectified can be one and the same person: A woman can become a sex object for herself, taking toward her own person the attitude of the man. She will then take erotic satisfaction in her physical self, reveling in her body as a beautiful object to be gazed at and decorated. Such an attitude is commonly called "narcissism," a term which received its baptism in psychoanalysis. In the most general sense, the narcissist, says Freud, "treats his [her] body in the same way as otherwise the body of a sexual object is treated."[11] Psychoanalysis, the most influential personality theory of modern times, has held not only that women are significantly more narcissistic than men (a finding which is, for us, compatible with the pervasive sexual objectification of women) but that narcissism is a necessary feature of the normal feminine personality. But how are we to understand such a claim? How is feminine narcissism possible, i.e., how is it possible for sexual objectification, which is profoundly alienating, to produce narcissistic states of consciousness, which are profoundly satisfying? We can understand the *interest* women have in conforming to the requirements of sexual objectification, given our powerlessness and dependency; less easy to explain is the *pleasure* we take in doing so.

In the next section, I shall examine the nature of feminine narcissism, an element of major significance in the psychic lives of women. While the term *narcissism* has come in recent years to have a very wide application, I shall restrict my use of the term to its original meaning in psychoanalytic parlance, namely, to an infatuation with one's bodily being. I do not intend by use of this term to refer to any personality disorder, but to an erotic disposition psychoanalytically trained observers and laypersons alike regard as typically female, to what in an older language would have been called "feminine vanity."[12] I shall try to show that feminine narcissism is not the rock on which the idea of femininity as alienation must founder. On the contrary, a fuller disclosure of this phenomenon can help to reveal the nature of a mode of self-estrangement which lies close to the heart of the feminine condition itself.

On Feminine Narcissism

Narcissism, for Freud, is our "primal psychic situation, the original disposition of libido. In the beginning, the

> ego's instincts are directed to itself and it is to some extent capable of deriving satisfaction for them on itself. This condition is known as narcissism and this potentiality for satisfaction is termed auto-erotic.[13]

Women, far more than men, are likely to remain in this "primal psychic situation," not surprisingly, since in the Freudian scheme of things, the female psyche is more archaic than the male. The explanatory device Freud uses to account for the greater proneness of women to self-admiration and bodily display is, of course, penis envy. Lacking the penis, young girls regard themselves as physically inferior to boys; feminine preoccupation with the body is an effort to compensate for an unconscious sense of physical deficiency.[14] In "On Narcissism,'' Freud takes note of the fact that feminine narcissism flowers in adolescence, but he makes an uncharacteristically crude effort to account for this:

> With the development of puberty the maturing of the female sexual organs, which up till then have been in a condition of latency, seem to bring about an intensification of the original narcissism.[15]

Helene Deutsch adds refinement to the favorite Freudian hypothesis. For her, feminine narcissism operates in the psyche as a counterweight to feminine masochism: The ''feminine woman . . . is characterized by her struggle for a harmonious accord between the narcissistic forces of self-love and the masochistic forces of dangerous and painful giving.''[16] While Deutsch does not express herself in quite this way, her meaning is clear: Narcissistic *eros* in woman binds masochistic *thanatos*. Without the antidote of self-love, woman would be helpless before the misfortunes an inherently masochistic nature will surely bring upon itself—as if a psychic constitution composed in such large measure of masochism and narcissism were not misfortune enough.

Neither psychoanalytic explanation is convincing. Narcissism in both sexes may have its origin in infantile eroticism, but Freudians cannot account for its perpetuation in women except by reference to the generally discredited theory of penis envy, or to the even more questionable notion of an innate death instinct. Existentialist literature provides a more satisfactory account of the persistence of feminine narcissism. Simone de Beauvoir makes use of the existentialist conception of ''situation'' in order to account for the persistence of narcissism in the feminine personality. A woman's situation, i.e., those meanings derived from the total context in which she comes to maturity, disposes her to apprehend her body not as the instrument of her transcendence, but as ''an object destined for another.''[17]

Knowing that she is to be subjected to the cold appraisal of the male connoisseur and that her life prospects may depend on how she is seen, a woman learns to appraise herself first. The sexual objectification of women produces a duality in feminine consciousness. The gaze of the Other is internalized so that I myself become at once seer and seen, appraiser and the thing appraised. The adolescent girl, just beginning to grasp the role she is to assume

> becomes an object and she sees herself as object; she discovers this new aspect of her being with surprise: it seems to her that she has been doubled; instead of coinciding exactly with herself, she now begins to exist outside.[18]

Narcissism, then, ''consists in the setting up of the ego as a double, a stranger.''[19] While the identity of this ''stranger'' has yet to be established, Beauvoir's language seems hyperbolic: The stranger who inhabits my consciousness is not really a stranger at all, but *myself.*

For both psychoanalysis and existentialism, narcissism is at once a source of profound satisfaction and a temptation to be resisted. For Beauvoir, the narcissist seeks to escape the burdens of subjectivity by identifying her entire self with her bodily self. Such a person wants to retain sufficient awareness to enjoy her own finished and perfect thinghood: She wishes, at one and the same time, to become that which partakes of the nature of consciousness (the *pour-soi*) as well as that which does not (the *en-soi*), but this is impossible.[20] On this analysis, the pleasures of narcissism arise from a self-deceived effort to escape the anguish of freedom.

For Freud, narcissistic satisfaction is not so metaphysical. "The first autoerotic sexual gratifications," he tells us, "are experienced in connection with vital functions in the service of self-preservation."[21] But narcissism is an *infantile* libido-position. As the ego develops, it is supposed to "cathect" its libido away from itself, to other persons and groups of persons, to work, in short, to the world. This series of cathexes, in ordinary parlance, is called "maturation." So the woman tempted by sexual objectification to persist in her narcissism will undergo a kind of psychological infantilization, the perfect intrapsychic parallel to that pervasive infantilization to which we are subject in the larger society: our enforced dependency; manufactured incompetence; weakness and helplessness; our traditional exclusion from many areas of adult life; the requirement not only that we act like children, but that we look like children too—smooth, soft, rounded, hairless and, above all, young.[22]

At this point, it might be tempting to say of many women that they simply prefer the reverent and self-absorbed pleasures of the mirror to the challenges of freedom, that narcissistic satisfaction ties us tightly to "femininity" and hence to false consciousness. But let us look more closely. In narcissism, the self undergoes doubling: An Other, a " stranger" who is at the same time myself, is subject for whom my bodily being is object. This Other may take on a number of identities—that of a remembered or fantasized parental regard; a significant male Other; even a self struggling toward self-actualization and a wholesome affirmation of the body. But very often this Other is an interiorized representative of what I shall call the "fashion-beauty complex." Like the "military-industrial complex," the fashion-beauty complex is a major articulation of capitalist patriarchy. While an analysis of this complex structure lies beyond the scope of this paper, it is a vast system of corporations—some of which manufacture products, others services and still others information, images, and ideologies—of emblematic public personages and of sets of techniques and procedures. As family and church have declined in importance as the central producers and regulators of "femininity," the fashion-beauty complex has grown.

Overtly, the fashion-beauty complex seeks to glorify the female body and to provide opportunities for narcissistic indulgence. More important than this is its *covert* aim, which is to depreciate woman's body and deal a blow to her narcissism. We are presented everywhere with images of perfect female beauty—at the drugstore cosmetics display, the supermarket magazine counter, on television. These images remind us constantly that we fail to measure up. Whose nose is the right shape, after all, whose hips are not too wide—or too narrow? The female body is revealed as a task, an object in need of transformation. "There are no ugly women," said Helena Rubinstein, "only lazy ones."[23] This project of transformation, as it is outlined in, e.g., *Vogue,* is daunting. Every aspect of my bodily being requires either alteration or else heroic measures merely to conserve it. The taboo on aging demands that I try to trap my body and remove it from time; in the feminine ideal of *stasis,* we find once more a source of women's physical passivity.

I must cream my body with a thousand creams, each designed to act against a different deficiency, oil it, pumice it, powder it, shave it, pluck it, depilate it, deodorize it, ooze it into just the right foundation, reduce it overall through spartan dieting or else pump it up with silicon. I must try to resculpture it on the ideal through dozens of punishing exercises. If home measures fail, I must take it to the figure salon, or inevitably, for those who can afford it, the plastic surgeon. There is no "dead time" in my day during which I do not stand under the imperative to improve myself: While waiting for the bus, I am to suck the muscles of my abdomen in and up to lend them "tone"; while talking on the telephone I am bidden to describe circles in the air with my feet to slim down my ankles. All these things must be done prior to the application of make-up, an art which aims, once again, to hide a myriad of deficiencies.

The fashion-beauty complex produces in woman an estrangement from her bodily being: On the one hand, she *is* it and is scarcely allowed to be anything else; on the other hand, she must exist perpetually at a distance from her physical self, fixed at this distance in a permanent posture of disapproval. Thus, insofar as the fashion-beauty complex shapes one of the introjected subjects for whom I exist as object, I sense myself as deficient. Nor am I able to control in any way those images which give rise to this sense of deficiency. Breasts are bound in one decade, padded in another. One season eyebrows are thick and heavy, the next pencil-thin. Not long ago, the mannequins in Marshall Field's windows were dressed in what appeared to be Victorian christening gowns; next season the "harlot look" was all the rage. Perhaps the most pervasive image of all, the one which dominates the pages of *Vogue,* is not an image of woman at all, but of a beautiful adolescent boy.[24] All the projections of the fashion-beauty complex have this in common: They are images of *what I am not.* For me, attention to the ordinary standards of hygiene are not enough; I am unacceptable as I am. We can now grasp the nature of feminine narcissism with more precision: It is *infatuation with an inferiorized body.* If this analysis is correct, narcissistic satisfaction is to some degree conditional upon a sense of successful adaptation to standards of feminine bodily presence generated by the enemies of women.

Earlier, I suggested the superiority of Beauvoir's account of feminine narcissism over standard Freudian explanations, not only because it stays clear of questionable theoretical constructions, e.g., of a death instinct, but because it takes cognizance of woman's situation in a way Freudian theory does not. Essential to this situation, as we have seen, is the experience of sexual objectification, which leads many women to a virtually irresistible introjection of the subject for whom they are object. Now, Beauvoir's account is certainly correct, but it is abstract and schematic. Narcissistic satisfaction is always *concrete*, i.e., it is experienced under circumstances which are historically specific. Beauvoir does not make clear the relationship of certain experienced satisfactions to the material base of contemporary capitalist society, to the way in which such satisfactions are manipulated or the extent to which agents of a complex, sophisticated, and immensely profitable corporate structure have taken up residence within the feminine psyche.[25]

While in its objective structure the fashion-beauty complex recalls the military-industrial complex, in its subjective effects, it bears comparison to the church. The church cultivates in its adherents very profound anxieties about the body, most particularly about bodily appetites and sexual desires. It then presents itself as the only instrument able, though expiation, to take away the very guilt and shame it has itself produced. The fashion-beauty complex refines and deepens feminine anxieties which would accompany the status of sex-object in any case; like the church, it offers itself, its procedures and institutions as uniquely able to diminish these anxieties. Magical physical transformations can be accomplished by the faithful like the spiritual transformations promised by the church: There is evidence, for example, that the physical qualities of cosmetics—their texture, color, and gloss—are incorporated into the actual body images of the women who use them. Body care rituals are like sacraments; at best, they put a woman who would be lost and abandoned without them into what may feel to her like a state of grace; at worst, they exhibit the typical obsessive-compulsive features of much religious behavior. Feminists are widely regarded as enemies of the family; we are also seen as enemies of the stiletto heel and the beauty parlor—in a word, as enemies of glamour. Hostility on the part of some women to feminism may have its origin here: The women's movement is seen not only to threaten profound sources of gratification and self-esteem but also to attack those rituals, procedures, and institutions upon which many women depend to lessen their sense of bodily deficiency.

The context within which we experience much narcissistic satisfaction bears the familiar marks of alienation. Earlier, I suggested that persons can be described as alienated or self-estranged if they suffer a splintering or fragmentation of such a nature as to prohibit the exercise of certain capacities the exercise of which is thought essential to a fully human existence. A truly "feminine" woman, then, has been seduced by a variety of cultural agencies into being a body not only for another, but for herself as well. But when this happens, she may well experience what is in effect a prohibition or a taboo on the development of her other human capacities: In our society, for example, the cultivation of intellect has made a woman not more but less sexually alluring. The fragmentation which women undergo in the process of sexual objectification is evident too: What occurs is not just the splitting of a person into mind and body but the splitting of the self into a number of personae, some who witness and some who are witnessed, and, if I am correct, some internal witnesses are in fact introjected representatives of agencies hostile to the self. Woman has lost control of the production of her own image, lost control to those whose production of these images is neither innocent nor benevolent, but obedient to imperatives which are both capitalist and phallocentric. In sum, women experience a twofold alienation in the production of our own persons: The beings we are to be are mere bodily beings; nor can we control the shape and nature these bodies are to take.

At the end of the first section of this essay, I posed this question: Is the claim that feminine narcissism involves self-estranged states of consciousness in any way compatible with the undeniable existence of narcissistic satisfaction? The shape of an answer has now emerged: The satisfactions of narcissism are real enough, but they are *repressive* satisfactions. "All liberation," says Marcuse, "depends on the consciousness of servitude and the emergence of this consciousness is always hampered by the predominance of needs and satisfactions which, to a great extent, have become the individual's own."[26] Repressive satisfaction fastens us to the established order of domination, for the same system which produces false needs also controls the conditions under which such needs can be satisfied. "False needs," it might be ventured, are needs which are produced through indoctrination, psychological manipulation, and the denial of autonomy; they are needs whose possession and satisfaction benefit not the subject who has them but a social order whose interest lies in domination. The price extracted for the satisfaction of repressive needs is high, for guilt, shame, and obsessional states of consciousness accompany the repressive satisfactions allowed us by the fashion-beauty complex. Repressive narcissistic satisfactions stand in the way of the emergence of an authentic delight in the body, too: The woman unable to leave home in the morning without "putting on her face" will never discover the beauty, character, and expressiveness her own face already possesses.

Coda: Toward a Nonrepressive Narcissism

If feminine narcissism is a major ingredient in what is ordinarily regarded as "femininity," and if certain manifestations of "femininity" can be construed as modes of alienation, then it follows that the de-alienation of woman's existence will require a struggle against that excessive, damaged, and debilitating narcissism which now holds sway. But having concluded this, we are at once confronted by a host of new questions. How, in the face of those distortions in our relationship to the body produced by the established order of domination, can we arrive at a concept of nonrepressive narcissism anyhow? If the struggle against sexual objectification is successful, to what extent will the narcissistic needs of women be reduced? Might they disappear entirely? But if there are ineradicable narcissistic needs after all, how might such needs be satisfied in ways which do not damage the self?

Feminist strategy in regard to these issues has taken a number of forms. There has not been a concerted attack on feminine narcissism, but on sexual objectification, its root. The necessity and urgency of such a campaign is beyond question. But feminist practice as a whole has not been consistent in this regard. Some segments of the movement have protested sexual objectification with little understanding of its internalized psychological consequences and with no repudiation either in theory or in practice of conventional standards of dress and appearance. Other women, in rebellion against objectification, have adopted a practice in which both body display and the need to be admired are taboo. But if there are legitimate narcissistic needs, such asceticism ignores them.

The women's movement has also put a very high priority on the development of the female body as instrument—on strength, agility, and physical competence. Training in self-defense and the campaign for equality in sports, in addition to their more immediate aims, open up to women new sources of self-esteem and satisfaction in embodiment. Struggles of this sort are indispensable, of course, but they do not exhaust what needs to be done, for we have consciousness of the body not only as instrument but as object for another as well; somatic awareness exists in both modes.

The interiorized witnesses to my bodily being do not form a harmonious unity: The contradictions which exist among them must be intensified. The personae who affirm the body must be strengthened. Those who are introjected representatives of agencies hostile to the self must be expelled from consciousness. The numerous exploitations of the fashion-beauty complex must be exposed at every opportunity and its idiotic image-mongering held up to a ridicule so relentless that that incorporation into the self on which it depends will become increasingly untenable.[27] As part of our practice, we must create a new witness, a collective significant Other, integrated into the self but nourished and strengthened from without, from a revolutionary feminist community. This collective Other, while not requiring body display, will not make it taboo either; it will allow and even encourage fantasy and play in self-ornamentation. Our ideas of the beautiful will have to be expanded and so altered that we will perceive ourselves and one another very differently than we do now. Much has been written about revolutionary aesthetics in connection with film, drama, and the visual arts, very little about a revolutionary aesthetic of the body. This is not surprising, since most revolutionary theory, in aesthetics as in other domains, has been the work of men, while the need for new ways of imagining the body is preeminently a need of women. The release of our capacity to apprehend the beautiful from the narrow limits within which it is now confined is part of what Marx meant, or should have meant, when he spoke in his most prophetic writing of an ''emancipation of the senses.''

4

Feminine Masochism and the
Politics of Personal Transformation

To be at once a sexual being and a moral agent can be troublesome indeed: no wonder philosophers have wished that we could be rid of sexuality altogether. What to do, for example, when the structure of desire is at war with one's principles? This is a difficult question for any person of conscience, but it has a particular poignancy for feminists. A prime theoretical contribution of the contemporary feminist analysis of women's oppression can be captured in the slogan "the personal is political." What this means is that the subordination of women by men is pervasive, that it orders the relationship of the sexes in every area of life, that a sexual politics of domination is as much in evidence in the private spheres of the family, ordinary social life, and sexuality as in the traditionally public spheres of government and the economy. The belief that the things we do in the bosom of the family or in bed are either "natural" or else a function of the personal idiosyncracies of private individuals is held to be an "ideological curtain that conceals the reality of women's systematic oppression."[1] For the feminist, two things follow upon the discovery that sexuality too belongs to the sphere of the political. The first is that whatever pertains to sexuality—not only actual sexual behavior, but sexual desire and sexual fantasy as well—will have to be understood in relation to a larger system of subordination; the second, that the deformed sexuality of patriarchical culture must be moved from the hidden domain of "private life" into an arena for struggle, where a "politically correct" sexuality of mutual respect will contend with an "incorrect" sexuality of domination and submission.

A number of questions present themselves at once. What is a politically correct sexuality, anyhow? What forms would the struggle for such a sexuality assume? Is it possible for individuals to prefigure more liberated forms of sexuality in their own lives now, in a society still marked by the subordination of women in every domain? Finally, the question with which we began, the moral worry about what to do when conscience and sexual desire come into conflict, will look like this when seen through the lens of feminism: What to do when one's own sexuality is "politically incorrect," when desire is wildly at variance with feminist principles? I turn to this question first.

The Story of P.

If any form of sexuality has a *prima facie* claim to be regarded as politically incorrect, it would surely be sadomasochism. I define sadomasochism as any sexual practice that involves the eroticization of relations of domination and submission. Consider the case of P., a feminist, who has masochistic fantasies. If P. were prepared to share her secret life with us, this is what she might say:

> For as long as I can remember (from around age six . . .), my sexual fantasies
> have involved painful exposure, embarrassment, humiliation, mutilation, domi-
> nation by Gestapo-like characters.[2]

P. regarded her fantasies as unnatural and perverse until she discovered that of all women who have sexual fantasies, 25 percent have fantasies of rape.[3] Indeed, much material which is often arousing to women, material not normally re-garded as perverse, is thematically similar to P.'s fantasies. Many women of her mother's generation were thrilled when the masterful Rhett Butler overpow-ered the struggling Scarlett O'Hara and swept her triumphantly upstairs in an act of marital rape: "treating 'em rough" has enhanced the sex appeal of many a male film star ever since.[4] The feminine taste for fantasies of victimization is assumed on virtually every page of the large pulp literature produced specifi-cally for women. Confession magazines, Harlequin romances, and that genre of historical romance known in the publishing trade as the "bodice-ripper" have sales now numbering in the billions, and they can be bought in most drugstores and supermarkets across the land. The heroes of these tales turn out to be nice guys in the end, but only in the end; before that they dominate and humiliate the heroines in small "Gestapo-like" ways. In the Harlequin romance *Moth to the Flame* (she the moth, he the flame), the hero, Santino, "whose mouth, despite its sensual curve looked as if it had never uttered the word 'compromise' in its life," insults the heroine, Juliet, mocks her, kidnaps her, steals her clothes, imprisons her in his seaside mansion in Sicily, and threatens repeatedly to rape her."[5] Ginny, the heroine of *Sweet Savage Love* is "almost raped, then almost seduced, then deflowered—half by rape and half by seduc-tion, then alternately raped and seduced"—all this by Steve, who is by turns her assailant and lover.[6] The purity and constancy of women like Juliet and Ginny finally restrain the brutality of their lovers and all ends happily in mar-riage, but one cannot escape the suspicion that the ruthlessness of these men constitutes a good part of their sex appeal. When at last brutality recedes and the couple is reconciled, the fantasy ends; *the story is over.*[7]

It might be ventured that standard heterosexual desire in women has often a masochistic dimension, though such desire would fall out far lower on a continuum of masochistic desire than P.'s fantasies or the average Harlequin romance. Essential to masochism is the eroticization of domination. Now women are regularly attracted by power, its possession and exercise. Male power manifests itself variously as physical prowess, muscular strength, intellectual brilliance, worldly position, or the kind of money that buys respect. One or another of these kinds of power may become erotically charged for a woman depending on her values, her history, or her personal idiosyncracies. In a sexually inegalitarian society, these manifestations of male power are precisely the instruments by which men are able to accomplish the subordination of women. Hence, insofar as male power is eroticized, male dominance itself becomes erotically charged.

One might object that there is nothing masochistic in the female attraction to power at all, that because the possession of power is a source of status for men, a woman who can attach herself to a powerful man will thereby enhance her own status. But this implies that the woman attracted by the athlete is aware only that his muscular prowess can protect her or gain him the esteem of his fellows, not that he can use it to restrain her if he wants, or that the student who idolizes her professor is unaware that he can use his stinging wit as much to put her down as to overawe his classes. I suggest instead that there is contained in the very apprehension of power the recognition that it can overwhelm and subdue as well as protect and impress. Power can raise me from my lowly status and exalt me; it is also that *before which I tremble.*

P. is deeply ashamed of her fantasies. Shame, according to John Deigh, is typically expressed in acts of concealment; it is a reaction to the threat of demeaning treatment one would invite in appearing to be a person of lesser worth.[8] P. would be mortified if her fantasies were somehow to be made public. But she suffers a continuing loss of esteem in her own eyes as well. While one of Schlafly's lieutenants might be embarrassed by such fantasies, too, P.'s psychic distress is palpable, for she feels obliged to play out in the theater of her mind acts of brutality which are not only abhorrent to her but which, as a political activist, she is absolutely committed to eradicating. She experiences her own sexuality as doubly humiliating; not only does the content of her fantasies concern humiliation but the very having of such fantasies, given her politics, is humiliating as well. Two courses of action seem open to someone in P.'s predicament; she can either get rid of her shame and keep her desire, or else get rid of her desire. I shall discuss each of these alternatives in turn.

Sadomasochism and Sexual Freedom

Sadomasochism has been roundly denounced in feminist writing, in particular the sadism increasingly evident in much male-oriented pornography.[9] Feminists have argued that sadomasochism is one inevitable expression of a women-hating culture. It powerfully reinforces male dominance and female subordination because, by linking these phenomena to our deepest sexual desires—desires defined by an ideologically tainted psychology as instinctual—it makes them appear natural. To participate willingly in this mode of sexuality is thus to collude in women's subordination. No wonder, then, that the emergence of Samois has shocked and offended many in the feminist community. Samois is an organization of and for sadomasochistic women which describes itself both as "lesbian" and "feminist."

In several recent publications, members of Samois have tried to justify their sexual tastes against the standard feminist condemnation. Women like P. are urged to set aside shame, to accept their fantasies fully, to welcome the sexual satisfaction such fantasies provide and even, in controlled situations, to act them out. Most manifestations of sexuality are warped anyhow, they argue, so why the particular scorn heaped upon sadomasochism? Why are the acts of sadomasochistic women—"negotiated mutual pleasure"—in which no one is really hurt worse than, e.g., conventional heterosexuality where the structure of desire in effect ties a woman erotically to her oppressor?[10] The critics of sadomasochism conflate fantasy and reality: Representations of violent acts should not be regarded with the same loathing as the acts themselves. Sadomasochism is ritual or theater in which the goings-on are entirely under the control of the actors; the participants are no more likely to want to engage in real acts of domination or submission than are the less sexually adventurous. Further, sadomasochism is liberatory, say its defenders, in that it challenges the sexual norms of the bourgeois family, norms still rooted to a degree in an older, more repressive sexual ethic that saw sexual acts as legitimate only if they were performed in the service of reproduction. Sadomasochism is the "quintessence of non-reproductive sex": its devotees have a "passion for making use of the entire body, every nerve fiber and every wayward thought."[11] Some members of Samois claim that there are moral values inherent in the sadomasochistic encounter itself, for example in the heightened trust the submissive member of a pair practicing bondage must have in the dominant member. An unusual attentiveness and sensitivity to the partner are required of one who has permission to inflict pain ("Good tops are the most compassionate and sensitive beings on earth"), while overt physical aggression "can function to keep a relationship clean," i.e.., free of festering guilt and psychological manipulation.[12]

Finally, sadomasochism is defended on general grounds of sexual freedom. Here, three arguments are brought forward. First, since sex is a basic human need and the right to seek sexual satisfaction is a basic human right, it follows that sexual freedom, in and of itself, is an intrinsic good, provided of course that the sexual activity in question is consensual. Second, the feminist condemnation of sadomasochism is said to be sexually repressive, perpetuating shame and secrecy in sexual matters and discouraging sexual experimentation and the exploration of unfamiliar terrain. Third, anything less than a total commitment to sexual freedom is said to endanger the future of the women's movement by giving ground to the newly militant Right. In the wake of its crusade against pornography, so say the women of Samois, the contemporary women's movement has abandoned its earlier commitment to sexual freedom and taken up positions that are clearly reactionary. Gayle Rubin, feminist anthropologist and leading Samois theorist, is highly critical of a recent resolution of the National Organization for Women which denies that sadomasochism, cross-generational sex, pornography, and public sex—unlike gay and lesbian sexuality—are issues of sexual or affectional preference which merit its support. For Rubin, this puts NOW on record as opposing sexual freedom and the civil rights of sexual nonconformists. Sexual freedom, she argues, is inextricable from political freedom. The rejection of persecuted and stigmatized erotic minorities plays into the hands of the conservative Right, which has been extraordinarily successful of late in tapping "pools of erotophobia in its accession to state power," power it uses, in turn, to consolidate its hold over many other kinds of erotic activity.[13]

How convincing is Samois's defense of sadomasochism? There is, first of all, some question whether the arguments they adduce are mutually consistent. It seems odd to insist that sadomasochistic practices are isolated and compartmentalized rituals which do not resonate with the rest of one's life activity and at the same time to claim that they can enhance the quality of ongoing real relationships, e.g., in the development of trust or the "clean" acting out of aggression. The claim that sadomasochism creates unique opportunities for the building of trust, while true in some sense, strikes me as peculiar. If someone—the "bottom"—allows herself to be tied helplessly to the bedpost, she must of course trust the one doing the tying up—the "top"—not to ignore whatever limits have been agreed upon in advance. If the bottom already knows her top and has reason to believe in her trustworthiness, how can this trust have come about except in the ordinary ways in which we all develop trust in intimate relationships? But if top and bottom are not well acquainted and the activity in question caps a chance meeting in a bar, the awarding of trust in such circumstances is an act of utter foolhardiness. Further, there is little consolation in the observation that sadomasochistic sexuality is no worse than the usual forms of sexuality under patriarchy. If true, this claim does not establish the allowability of sadomasochism at all but only highlights once more the thoroughgoing corruption of much of what we do and the urgent need for a radical revision of erotic life. Nor can sadomasochistic sexuality be justified solely on the grounds that it is frequently non-procreative or that it violates the norms of the bourgeois family, for there are morally reprehensible practices, e.g., necrophilia, which shock respectable people too and are non-procreative into the bargain.[14]

I agree entirely with Gayle Rubin's demand that feminists defend sexual freedom, most tested in the case of sexual minorities, against a newly militant Right. But a political movement may defend some type of erotic activity against prudery or political conservatism without implying in any way that the activity in question is mandated by or even consistent with its own principles. Prostitution is a case in point. There are reasons, in my view, why feminists ought to support the decriminalization of prostitution. If prostitution were legalized, prostitutes would no longer be subject to police or Mafia shakedowns or to the harassment of fines and imprisonment, nor would they need the protection of pimps who often brutalize them. However, none of this implies approval of prostitution as an institution or an abandonment of the feminist vision of a society without prostitutes.

The most convincing defense of sadomasochism, no doubt, is the claim that since sexual satisfaction is an intrinsic good, we are free to engage in any sexual activities whatsoever, provided of course that these activities involve neither force nor fraud. But this is essentially a *liberal* response to a *radical* critique of sexuality and, as such, it fails entirely to engage this critique. As noted earlier, one of the major achievements of contemporary feminist theory is the recognition that male supremacy is perpetuated not only openly, through male domination of the major societal institutions, but more covertly, through the manipulation of desire. Moreover, desires may be produced and managed in ways which involve neither force nor fraud nor the violation of anyone's legal rights. Elsewhere, none other than Gayle Rubin herself has described the "sex-gender system," that complex process whereby bi-sexual infants are transformed into male and female gender personalities, the one destined to command, the other to obey:

> While particular socio-sexual systems vary, each one is specific and individuals within it will have to conform to a finite set of possibilities. Each new generation must learn and become its sexual destiny, each person must be encoded with its appropriate status within the system.[15]

From this perspective, the imposition of masculinity and femininity may be regarded as a process of organizing and shaping desire. The truly "feminine" woman, then, will have "appropriate" sexual desires for men, but she will wish to shape herself, physically and in other ways, into a woman men will desire. Thus, she will aspire to a life-plan proper for a member of her sex, to a certain ideal configuration of the body and to an appropriate style of self-presentation. The idea that sexual desire is a kind of bondage is very ancient; the notion takes on new meaning in the context of a radical feminist critique of male supremacy.

The "perverse" behavior defended by Rubin and the other members of Samois is clearly not identical to "ordinary" feminine masochism, to that masochism so characteristic of women that it has been regarded by all psychoanalysts and many feminists as one of the typical marks of femininity in this culture.[16] But it is not so very different either. The "normal" and the "perverse" have in common the sexualization of domination and submission, albeit to different degrees. Feminine masochism, like femininity in general, is an economical way of embedding women in patriarchy through the mechanism of desire, and while the eroticization of relations of domination may not lie at the heart of the system of male supremacy, it surely perpetuates it. The precise mechanisms at work in the sexualization of domination are unclear, and it would be difficult to show in every case a connection between a particular sexual act or sexual fantasy and the oppression of women in general. While it would be absurd to claim that women accept less pay than men because it is sexually exciting to earn sixty-two cents for every dollar a man earns, it would be equally naive to insist that there is no relationship whatever between erotic domination and sexual subordination. Surely women's acceptance of domination by men cannot be entirely independent of the fact that for many women, *dominance in men is exciting*.

The right, staunchly defended by liberals, to desire what and whom we please and, under certain circumstances, to act on our desire, is not an issue here; the point is that women would be better off if we learned when to refrain from the exercise of this right. A thorough overhaul of desire is clearly on the feminist agenda: the fantasy that we are overwhelmed by Rhett Butler should be traded in for one in which we seize state power and reeducate him. P. has no choice, then, except to reject the counsel of Samois that, unashamed, she make space in her psyche for the free and full enjoyment of every desire. Samois in effect advises P. to ignore in her own life a general principle to which, as a feminist, she is committed and which she is therefore bound to represent to all other women: the principle that we struggle to decolonize our sexuality by removing from our minds the internalized forms of oppression that make us easier to control.

In their enthusiasm for sexual variation, liberals ignore the extent to which a person may experience her own sexuality as arbitrary, hateful, and alien to the rest of her personality. Each of us is in pursuit of an inner integration and unity, a sense that the various aspects of the self form a harmonious whole. But when the parts of the self are at war with one another, a person may be said to suffer from self-estrangement. That part of P. which is compelled to produce sexually charged scenarios of humiliation is radically at odds with the P. who devotes much of her life to the struggle against oppression. Now perfect consistency is demanded of no one, and our little inconsistencies may even lend us charm. But it is no small thing when the form of desire is disavowed by the personality as a whole. The liberal is right to defend the value of sexual satisfaction, but the struggle to achieve an integrated personality has value too and the liberal position does not speak to those situations in which the price of sexual satisfaction is the perpetuation of self-estrangement.

Phenomenologists have argued that affectivity has a cognitive dimension, that emotions offer a certain access to the world. P.'s shame, then, is the reflection in affectivity of a recognition that there are within her deep and real divisions. Insofar as these divisions cannot be reconciled—the one representing stubborn desire, the other a passionate political commitment—there is a sense in which P. is entitled to her shame. Now this is *not* to say that P. *ought* to feel shame: Profound existential contradictions are not uncommon and our response to them may vary. But it seems equally mistaken to claim that P. ought not to feel what she feels. Her desires are not worthy of her, after all, nor is it clear that she is a mere helpless victim of patriarchal conditioning, unable to take any responsibility at all for her wishes and fantasies.

It is often the case that the less unwanted desires are acknowledged as belonging to the self and the more they are isolated and compartmentalized, the more psychic distress is minimized. The more extreme the self-estrangement, in other words, the less intense the psychic discomfort. P.'s shame and distress may well be a sign that she is *not* reconciled to her lack of inner harmony and integration and that she clings to the hope that the warring factions within her personality will still somehow be reconciled.

The Strangest Alchemy: Pain into Pleasure

If P. is not well advised just to keep her desires, getting rid of them seems to be the obvious alternative. Now it seems reasonable to assume that an unwelcome thought, e.g., an obsession, might be banished more easily from the mind if one could learn how it got there in the first place. What, then, are the causes of masochism? Two difficulties present themselves at the outset.

First, writers in the psychoanalytic tradition have used the term *masochism* to refer to anything from the self-chosen martyrdom of Simone Weil to the bizarre rituals of the leather fetishist, from the hysteric who uses an illness to manipulate those around her to the cabinet minister who pays a prostitute to whip him. Second, even a cursory review of the psychological literature turns up a bewildering array of theories. For the sake of simplicity, let us restrict our investigation to theories of masochism which focus on feminine masochism in particular.

Freud and the early psychoanalysts never doubted that the female nature was inherently masochistic.[17] They believed masochism in women to be largely instinctual in origin, i.e., the consequence of a certain channeling of libido away from its earlier "active-sadistic" clitoral "cathexis" to a "passive-masochistic" investment in the vagina. What does this mean? A "narcissistic wound" is suffered by the girl when she discovers the "inferiority" of her own organ; this causes her to turn away in disappointment from her "immature" clitoral investment and from active self-stimulation of her own body. She then begins to anticipate fulfillment first from the father, then, much later, from his representative. Since the potential of the vagina for sexual pleasure is awakened only by penetration, the psychosexually mature women, fit for heterosexual intercourse and hence for the reproduction of the species, must wait to be chosen and then "taken" by the male. The repression of clitoral sexuality is necessary if this is to happen.[18]

The eminent Freudian Helene Deutsch believed that since menstruation, defloration, and childbirth—the principal events in the sexual lives of women—are painful, feminine masochism is functionally necessary for the preservation of the species.[19] Marie Bonaparte believed that the idea of intercourse causes the girl to fear attack to the inside of her body; only the transformation from the active-sadistic to the passive-masochistic libido can allow a woman to accept the "continual laceration of sexual intercourse."[20] Sandor Rado, another Freudian, believed that the extreme mental pain suffered by the girl when she discovers her "castration" excites her sexually; hereafter she can only attain sexual satisfaction through suffering.[21] This seems counter-intuitive: Why should the trauma of an imagined castration be sexually exciting? In a later and more convincing attempt to account for the eroticization of suffering, Rado tries to show how some pains can become pleasures: The pain the masochist seeks is expiation, the pleasure the license purchased by pain to gratify forbidden desires.[22] The idea that sexual guilt is the key to an understanding of masochism is a common thread that connects a variety of theories of masochism and appears to be favored by the very few feminists who have had something to say on the topic. Women are taught to be more inhibited and guilty about their sexual desires than are men; hence the greater proneness of women to masochism. Rape and bondage fantasies, in particular, are said to allow a woman to imagine herself engaged in wicked but intensely pleasurable activities without any connivance on her part whatsoever; pleasure, so to speak, must be inflicted upon her.[23]

Adolf Grunberger believes that women have a guilty fantasy of stealing the penis: "Women pretend to offer themselves entirely, in place of the stolen penis proposing that the partner do to her body, to her ego, to herself, what she had in fantasy done to his penis."[24] Here the principal mechanism at work seems not so much the need to expiate the sin of sexual desire, but the displacement of aggression: Hostility aimed at first outward toward another, gets turned round upon the self. Social constraints, fear of punishment, or else guilt in the face of one's own anger (especially when the parents are its object) make it unsafe to vent aggressive feelings against anyone but oneself. Theodore Reik, in particular, is associated with the view that masochism in both sexes is frustrated sadism. Since our system of social conventions allows men more freedom to vent their anger, it is no wonder that the masochistic disposition is observed more frequently in the female.[25]

The same phenomenon—feminine masochism—is ascribed by Melanie Klein to infantile hatred for the mother and by Helle Thorning, a contemporary feminist psychologist, to desire to merge with the mother. According to Klein, when the little girl finds that the mother cannot satisfy all her desires, she turns away from the "bad" maternal breast—the symbol of libidinal frustration—and seeks a "good object"—the father—who will furnish her with the "object-oriented and narcissistic satisfactions she lacks."[26] Her second object, the father, will be idealized in proportion to the child's disappointment in her first object—the mother. Because of this, the girl will have to repress and, in psychoanalytic jargon, "countercathect" the aggression which exists in her relation to the father: The anal-sadistic desire for the penis is thus changed into the typical passive-masochistic posture of the "feminine" woman. A number of themes are brought together in this account: penis envy, incestuous fantasy, the helplessness and dependency of the child, and the inhibition of infantile aggression. Thorning starts from the same premise, i.e., the child's total dependency upon the maternal caregiver. But for her, feminine masochism, female passivity, and the fear of independent action in general represent an incomplete individuation from the mother, the failure to achieve an independent identity. The fantasy of total powerlessness is really an attempt to achieve oneness once more with the omnipotent caretaker of early childhood.[27] This sampling of psychoanalytic theories of masochism should not obscure the fact that there are non-psychoanalytic theories as well. George Bataille has produced a neo-Hegelian theory of erotic violation, while Sartre and Simone de Beauvoir believe that masochism is a self-deceived hence futile effort to turn oneself into an object for another in order to escape the "anguish" of freedom and the frightening evanescence of consciousness.[28]

What is P. to make of this chaos of theories? Indeed, what are *we* to make of it? Which account best explains that perverse alchemy at the heart of masochism—the transformation of pain into pleasure? Is it possible that the variety of things that go by the name of masochism are really multiple effects of multiple causes and that each theory captures something of what went on sometime, somewhere, in the psychosexual development of someone? To whom ought P. to turn for advice? What Sartre tells us in regard to the choice of a moral authority is true of the choice of a psychotherapeutic "expert" as well, namely, that the decision to whom to turn for advice is already a decision about what sort of advice we are prepared to take.

Let us suppose that P., determined to bring her desires into line with her ideology, embarks upon a course of traditional psychotherapy, and let us further suppose that her psychotherapy is unsuccessful. As part of her political education, P. is now exposed to a radical critique of psychotherapy: Psychotherapy is sexist; it is authoritarian and hierarchical; it is mired in the values of bourgeois society. P. now resolves to consult a "politically correct" therapist, indeed, a feminist therapist. In order to bring our discussion forward, let us suppose that this second attempt is unsuccessful too, for in spite of its popularity there is evidence that therapy fails as often as it succeeds, whatever the theoretical orientation of the therapist.[29] P. is finding it no simple thing to change her desires. Ought she to try again? In a society with little cohesiveness and less confidence in its own survival, an obsessional preoccupation with self has come to replace more social needs and interests. For many people, there is no higher obligation than to the self—to get it "centered", to realize its "potentialities," to clear out its "hangups"—and little to life apart from a self-absorbed trek through the fads, cults, and therapies of our time. But how compatible is such a surrender to the "new narcissism" (the old "bourgeois individualism") with a serious commitment to radical reform? Few but the relatively privileged can afford psychotherapy anyhow, and the search for what may well be an unrealizable ideal of mental health can absorb much of a person's time, energy, and money. It is not at all clear that the politically correct course of action for P. is to continue in this way whatever the cost; perhaps she is better advised to direct her resources back toward the women's movement. She is, after all, not psychologically disabled; within the oppressive realities of the contemporary world, her life is richer and more effective than the lives of many other people, and she is reconciled to her life—in every respect but one.

Paradise Lost and Not Regained: The Failure of a Politics of Personal Transformation

The view is widespread among radical feminists, especially among certain lesbian separatists, that female sexuality is malleable and diffuse and that a woman can, if she chooses, alter the structure of her desire. Here then is a new source of moral instruction for P., a source at the opposite pole from Samois. Without the help of any paid professional—for no such help is really needed— P. is now to pull herself up by her own psychological bootstraps.

The idea that we can alter our entire range of sexual feelings I shall call "sexual voluntarism." Sexual voluntarism has two sources: first, the fact that for many women, thoroughgoing and unforeseen personal changes, including the rejection of heterosexuality for lesbian sexuality, have often accompanied the development of a feminist politics; second, a theory of sexuality that relies heavily on Skinnerian-style behaviorism. While it is a fact that many women (and even some men) have been able to effect profound personal transformations under the influence of feminist ideas, a theory of sexuality I believe to be both false and politically divisive has taken this fact as evidence for the practicability of a willed transformation of self.

For the sexual voluntarist, individuals are thought to be blank tablets on which the culture inscribes certain patterns of behavior. Sexual norms are embedded in a variety of cultural forms, among them "common sense," religion, the family, books, magazines, television, films, and popular music. Individuals are "positively reinforced," i.e., rewarded, when they model their behavior on images and activities held out to them as normal and desirable, "negatively reinforced", i.e., punished, when their modeling behavior is done incorrectly or not done at all.

> If we come to view male-dominated heterosexuality as the only healthy form
> of sex, it is because we are bombarded with that model for our sexual fantasies
> long before we experience sex itself. Sexual images of conquest and submission
> pervade our imagination from an early age and determine how we will later
> look upon and experience sex.[30]

The masters of patriarchal society make sure that the models set before us
incorporate their needs and preferences: All other possibilities become unspeak-
able or obscene. Thus, the pervasiveness of propaganda for heterosexuality, for
female passivity, and male sexual aggressivity are responsible not only for
ordinary heterosexuality but for sadomasochism as well. Sadomasochists reveal
to the world, albeit in an exaggerated form, the inner nature of heterosexuality
and they are stigmatized by the larger society precisely because they tear the
veil from what patriarchal respectability would like to hide.[31] Sadomasochism is

> a conditioned response to the sexual imagery that barrages women in this
> society. . . . It is not surprising that women respond physically and emotion-
> ally to sadomasochistic images. Whether a woman identifies with the dominant
> or submissive figure in the fantasy, she is still responding to a model of sexual
> interaction that has been drummed into us throughout our lives.[32]

The language of these passages is graphic and leaves little doubt as to the theory
of sexuality which is being put forward. Models of sexual relationship bombard
us: they are drummed into our heads: the ideological apparatus of patriarchal
society is said to condition the very structure of desire itself.

What is valuable in this view is the idea that sexuality is socially constructed.
But are the voluntarists right about the mode of its construction? And those
patterns of desire which may have been present in a person's psyche from the
virtual dawn of consciousness: Are voluntarists perhaps too sanguine about the
prospects of radically altering these patterns in adult life? (See Section V below.)
Writing in *Signs*, Ethel Spector Person denies the ability of theories like this to
account for sexual deviance; why it is, for example, that fully 10 percent of the
American population is said to be exclusively homosexual, in spite of incessant
bombardment by propaganda for heterosexuality.[33] Quite early in life, many
people discover unusual sexual predilections which have been "modeled" for
them by no one. "I thought I was the only one," such people say, when
they "come out," enter psychoanalysis, or write their memoirs. Furthermore,
deviance rarely goes unpunished: Punishments may range from a purely private
embarrassment before the spectacle of one's own fantasy life to electric shock,
the stake, or the concentration camp. Indeed, the history of sexual deviance,
insofar as this history is known at all, is the history of the failure of massive
negative reinforcement to establish an absolute hegemony of the "normal."

One can deviate from a feminist standard of sexual behavior as well as from the obligatory heterosexuality of the larger society. Given their theoretical commitments, feminist sexual voluntarists are unable to regard departure from feminist sexual norms as due to anything but a low level of political understanding on the one hand, or to weakness of will on the other or, of course, to a little of both.[34] They reason that if our sexuality is in fact a product of social conditioning, then we can become ourselves our own social conditioners and programmers, substituting a feminist input for a patriarchal one. Failure to do this is made out to fear, or insufficient determination, or not trying hard enough, i.e., to some form of *akrasia* or else to an inability to comprehend the extent to which certain patterns of sexual behavior—for example, sadomasochism or heterosexuality—support the patriarchal order. The feminist analysis of sexuality has, quite correctly, been a major theoretical achievement of the Second Wave; crucial to this analysis is an understanding of the extent to which our sexuality has been colonized. Hence, the refusal or inability of a woman to bring her sexuality into conformity is a serious matter indeed and may tend, in the eyes of many, to diminish her other contributions to the women's movement, whatever they may be. This kind of thinking has led to painful divisions within the radical women's movement. The accused, guilt-ridden heterosexuals or closeted masochists, stand charged with lack of resolve, inconsistency, or even collusion with the enemy, while their accusers adopt postures of condescension or self-righteousness.

"Any woman can"—such is the motto of voluntarism. Armed with an adequate feminist critique of sexuality and sufficient will power, any women should be able to alter the pattern of her desires. While the feminist theory needed for this venture is known to be the product of collective effort, and while groups of women—even, in the case of lesbian separatism, organized communities of women—may be waiting to welcome the reformed pervert, the process of transformation is seen, nonetheless, as something a woman must accomplish alone. How can it be otherwise, given the fact that no tendency within the contemporary women's liberation movement has developed a genuinely collective *praxis* which would make it possible for women like P. to bring their desires into line with their principles? (I shall return to this point later.) A pervasive and characteristic feature of bourgeois ideology has here been introduced into feminist theory, namely, the idea that the victims, the colonized, are responsible for their own colonization and that they can change the circumstances of their lives by altering their consciousness. Of course, no larger social transformation can occur unless individuals change as well, but the tendency I am criticizing places the burden for effecting change squarely upon the individual, an idea quite at variance with radical feminist thinking generally.

One final point, before I turn to another mode of theorizing about sexuality—one not as subject to moralism and divisiveness. Those who claim that any woman can reprogram her consciousness if only she is sufficiently determined hold a shallow view of the nature of patriarchal oppression. Anything done can be undone, it is implied; nothing has been permanently damaged, nothing irretrievably lost. But this is tragically false. One of the evils of a system of oppression is that it may damage people in ways that cannot always be undone. Patriarchy invades the intimate recesses of personality where it may maim and cripple the spirit forever. No political movement, even a movement with a highly developed analysis of sexual oppression, can promise an end to sexual alienation or a cure for sexual dysfunction. Many human beings, P. among them, may have to live with a degree of psychic damage that can never be fully healed.

Sex-prints, Microdots, and the Stubborn Persistence of the Perverse

The difficulties individuals experience in trying to propel themselves, through "will power" or various therapies into more acceptable modes of sexual desire may be due to a connection between sexuality and personal identity too complex and obscure to be contained within the simple schemas of determinism. Ethel Spector Person has suggested that the relationship between sexuality and identity is mediated not only by gender, but by what she calls the "sex-print." The sex-print is "an individualized script that elicits erotic desire," an "individual's erotic signature." [35] Because it is experienced not as chosen but as revealed, an individual script is normally felt to be deeply rooted, "deriving from one's nature," unchanging and unique, somewhat like a fingerprint. Person does not claim that one's sex-print is absolutely irreversible, only relatively so, in part because the learning of a sex-print is so connected to the process of identity formation. "To the degree that an individual utilizes sexuality (for pleasure, for adaptation, as the resolution of unconscious conflict) . . . one's sexual 'nature' will be experienced as more or less central to personality."[36] In other words, what I take to be my "self" is constituted in large measure by certain patterns of response—to the events that befall me, to other people, even to inanimate nature. Thus, if someone asks me what I am like and I describe myself as aggressive, or ambitious, or fun-loving, I am naming certain modes of adaptation that capture who I am. Since sexuality is a major mode of response—a way of inhabiting the body as well as entering into relationships with others—patterns of sexual response may well be central to the structure of a person's identity.

Person suspects some factors that may be involved in psychosexual development. Following Chodorow, she grants that the larger observed differences between male and female sex-prints may be due to the differing outcomes of virtually universal female mothering for boy and girl children. Repression and fixation play a role too, as does the general structure of the family in modern patriarchal society and one's own family romance in particular. "Direct cultural proscriptions" (including that ideological conditioning discussed in Section IV) have some influence too, though "such strictures are not usually decisive in psychological life."[37] The fact that sexual excitement is so often tied to ideas of domination and submission may be due to the fact that sensual feelings develop in the helpless child, dependent not only for gratification but for its very survival on powerful adults.[38]

The psychoanalyst Robert Stoller characterizes the individualized sexual script not as a "sex-print" but as a "microdot," a highly compressed and encoded system of information out of which can be read—by one who knows how to read it—the history of a person's psychic life. Stoller regards as central to a person's sexual scenario the history of her infantile sexual traumas and her concomitant feelings of rage and hatred. Of the various modes of adaptation and response that get inscribed in the sex-print or microdot,

> it is hostility—the desire, overt or hidden, to harm another person—that gener-
> ates and enhances sexual excitement . . . . The exact details of the script under-
> lying the excitement are meant to reproduce and repair the precise traumas and
> frustrations—debasements—of childhood.[39]

Theories of the microdot and sex-print provide an alternative to the Skinnerian-style behaviorism of some radical feminists. While they remain within the psychoanalytic mode, these formulations nonetheless avoid the arbitrariness and excessive speculation so characteristic of earlier psychoanalytic theories. More general than the earlier theories, they are, in a sense, less informative, but their weakness in this regard may turn out to be an advantage. One suspects that many classical psychoanalytic theories (including some I examined earlier) are based on little more than an extrapolation from the analysis of a very few patients. Theories of this sort may well be subsumable under the more general formulations put forward by Person and Stoller, for the tales of psychosexual development told by these older theories may represent nothing more than the analyst's reading of the microdots of a limited range of patients.

There exists a substantial theoretical literature on the subject of human psychosexual development. Taken as a whole, this literature is confusing and often contradictory. While highly provocative and at times extraordinarily illuminating, much of it is methodologically suspect, lacks an adequate empirical foundation, and is often grounded in systems of ideas, e.g., Freudian psychology, which continue to generate enormous controversy. While some factors involved in the genesis of a sexual script have surely been identified, albeit in a very general way, Ethel Spector Person can still judge, correctly, I think, that "the mechanism of sex-printing is obscure" and that the connection between the learning of a sexual scenario and the process of identity formation remains mysterious.[40]

Whatever the precise mechanisms involved in the formation of a sex-print, it seems clear to me that each of us has one and that feminist theorists have focused far too much on the larger and more general features of a scenario such as a person's sexual orientation and too little on its "details." Does a person favor promiscuity or monogamy, for example, sex with "irrelevant" fantasies or sex without them, sex with partners of her own or of another race? People with the "wrong" kind of sexual orientation suffer a special victimization in our society; nevertheless, less dramatic features of the sex-print may be quite as saturated with meaning and just as revelatory of the basic outlines of a personality; the fact, for example, that Portnoy desires only gentile women is not less important in understanding *who he is* than the fact that he desires women.

Stoller has written that the history of a person's psychic life lies hidden in her or his sexual script. This history and the meanings which compose it can sometimes be read out of someone's scenario but often as not, it is shrouded in mystery—as P., to her sorrow, has already learned. Is Portnoy's attraction to gentile women a manifestation of Jewish self-hatred? Or a feeble attempt to deceive the superego about the real object of desire, his mother—a Jewish woman? Or, by picking women with whom he has little in common, is Portnoy acting on a masochistic need to be forever unhappy in love? The pattern of Portnoy's desire may reflect a mode of adaptation to the conflict and pain of early life, to a buried suffering Portnoy can neither recover nor surmount.

Sexual desire may seize and hold the mind with the force of an obsession, even while we remain ignorant of its origin and meaning. Arbitrary and imperious, desire repels not only rational attempts to explain it but all too often the efforts of rational individuals to resist it. At the level of theory the lack of an adequate account of the mechanisms involved in sex-printing (and hence of sadomasochism) is a failure of *science;* at the level of personal experience, the opacity of human sexual desire represents a failure of *self-knowledge.*

Instead of a Conclusion

P. will search the foregoing discussion in vain for practical moral advice. The way out of her predicament seemed to be the abandonment either of her shame or of her desire. But I have suggested that there is a sense in which she is "entitled" to her shame, insofar as shame is a wholly understandable response to behavior which is seriously at variance with principles. In addition, I have argued that not every kind of sexual behavior, even behavior that involves consenting adults or is played out in the private theater of the imagination, is compatible with feminist principles, a feminist analysis of sexuality, or a feminist vision of social transformation. To this extent, I declare the incompatibility of a classical liberal position on sexual freedom with my own understanding of feminism.

P.'s other alternative, getting rid of her desire, is a good and sensible project if she can manage it, but it turns out to be so difficult in the doing that to preach to her a feminist code of sexual correctness in the confident anticipation that she will succeed would be a futility—and a cruelty. Since many women (perhaps even most women) are in P.'s shoes, such a code would divide women within the movement and alienate those outside of it. "Twix't the conception and creation," writes the poet, "falls the shadow." Between the conception of a sexuality in harmony with feminism and the creation of a feminist standard of political correctness in sexual matters, fall not one but two shadows: first, the lack of an adequate theory of sexuality; the second the lack of an effective political practice around issues of personal transformation. The second shadow need not wait upon the emergence of the first, for to take seriously the principle of the inseparability of theory and practice is to see that a better theoretical understanding of the nature of sexual desire might well begin to emerge in the course of a serious and sustained attempt to alter it.

I am not suggesting that human sexuality is entirely enigmatic. Quite the contrary. There have been revolutionary advances in our knowledge of human sexual psychology over the last ninety years, and the work of feminist theorists such as Nancy Chodorow, Esther Person, and Dorothy Dinnerstein promises to extend our understanding still further. Nor do I want to substitute a sexual determinism for sexual voluntarism. Some people try to reorganize their erotic lives and they succeed. Others, caught up in the excitement of a movement that calls for the radical transformation of every human institution, find that they have changed without even trying. But more often than not, sexuality is mysterious and opaque, seemingly unalterable because its meaning is impenetrable. The significance of a particular form of desire as well as its persistence may lie in a developmental history only half-remembered or even repressed altogether. However embarrassing from a feminist perspective, a tabooed desire may well play a crucial and necessary role in a person's psychic economy.

The order of the psyche, here and now, in a world of pain and oppression, is not identical to the ideal order of a feminist political vision. We can teach a woman how to plan a demonstration, how to set up a phone bank, or how to lobby. We can share what we have learned about starting up a women's studies program or a battered women's shelter. But we cannot teach P. or the women of Samois or even ourselves how to decolonize the imagination: This is what I meant earlier by the claim that the women's movement has an insufficiently developed practice around issues of sexuality. The difficulties which stand in the way of the emergence of such a practice are legion; another paper would be required to identify them and also to examine the circumstances in which many women and some men have been able to effect dramatic changes in their lives. But in my view, the prevalence in some feminist circles of the kind of thinking I call "sexual voluntarism," with its simplistic formulas, moralism, intolerance, and refusal to acknowledge the obsessional dimension of sexual desire, is itself an obstacle to the emergence of an adequate practice.

Those who find themselves in the unfortunate situation of P. are living out, in the form of existential unease, contradictions which are present in the larger society. I refer to the contradiction between our formal commitment to justice and equality on the one hand—a commitment that the women's movement is determined to force the larger society to honor—and the profoundly authoritarian character of our various systems of social relationships on the other. Those who have followed my ''Story of P.'' will have to decide whether P. is in fact caught in a historical moment which we have not as yet surpassed or whether I have merely written a new apology for a very old hypocrisy.

5

Foucault, Femininity, and the Modernization of Patriarchal Power

I

In a striking critique of modern society, Michel Foucault has argued that the rise of parliamentary institutions and of new conceptions of political liberty was accompanied by a darker counter-movement, by the emergence of a new and unprecedented discipline directed against the body. More is required of the body now than mere political allegiance or the appropriation of the products of its labor: The new discipline invades the body and seeks to regulate its very forces and operations, the economy and efficiency of its movements.

The disciplinary practices Foucault describes are tied to peculiarly modern forms of the army, the school, the hospital, the prison, and the manufactory; the aim of these disciplines is to increase the utility of the body, to augment its forces:

> What was then being formed was a policy of coercions that act upon the body, a calculated manipulation of its elements, its gestures, its behaviour. The human body was entering a machinery of power that explores it, breaks it down and rearranges it. A 'political anatomy', which was also a 'mechanics of power', was being born; it defined how one may have a hold over others' bodies, not only so that they may do what one wishes, but so that they may operate as one wishes, with the techniques, the speed and the efficiency that one determines. Thus, discipline produces subjected and practiced bodies, 'docile' bodies.[1]

The production of "docile bodies" requires that an uninterrupted coercion be directed to the very processes of bodily activity, not just their result; this "micro-physics of power" fragments and partitions the body's time, its space, and its movements.[2]

The student, then, is enclosed within a classroom and assigned to a desk he cannot leave; his ranking in the class can be read off the position of his desk in the serially ordered and segmented space of the classroom itself. Foucault tells us that "Jean-Baptiste de la Salle dreamt of a classroom in which the spatial distribution might provide a whole series of distinctions at once, according to the pupil's progress, worth, character, application, cleanliness, and parents' fortune."[3] The student must sit upright, feet upon the floor, head erect; he may not slouch or fidget; his animate body is brought into a fixed correlation with the inanimate desk.

The minute breakdown of gestures and movements required of soldiers at drill is far more relentless:

> Bring the weapon forward. In three stages. Raise the rifle with the right hand, bringing it close to the body so as to hold it perpendicular with the right knee, the end of the barrel at eye level, grasping it by striking it with the right hand, the arm held close to the body at waist height. At the second stage, bring the rifle in front of you with the left hand, the barrel in the middle between the two eyes, vertical, the right hand grasping it at the small of the butt, the arm outstretched, the triggerguard resting on the first finger, the left hand at the height of the notch, the thumb lying along the barrel against the moulding. At the third stage. . . .[4]

These "body-object articulations" of the soldier and his weapon, the student and his desk, effect a "coercive link with the apparatus of production." We are far indeed from older forms of control that "demanded of the body only signs or products, forms of expression or the result of labour."[5]

The body's time, in these regimes of power, is as rigidly controlled as its space: The factory whistle and the school bell mark a division of time into discrete and segmented units that regulate the various activities of the day. The following timetable, similar in spirit to the ordering of my grammar school classroom, was suggested for French "écoles mutuelles" of the early nineteenth century:

> 8:45 entrance of the monitor, 8:52 the monitor's summons, 8:56 entrance of the children and prayer, 9:00 the children go to their benches, 9:04 first slate, 9:08 end of dictation, 9:12 second slate, etc.[6]

Control this rigid and precise cannot be maintained without a minute and relentless surveillance.

Jeremy Bentham's design for the Panopticon, a model prison, captures for Foucault the essence of the disciplinary society. At the periphery of the Panopticon, a circular structure; at the center, a tower with wide windows that opens onto the inner side of the ring. The structure on the periphery is divided into

5

Foucault, Femininity, and the Modernization of Patriarchal Power

I

In a striking critique of modern society, Michel Foucault has argued that the rise of parliamentary institutions and of new conceptions of political liberty was accompanied by a darker counter-movement, by the emergence of a new and unprecedented discipline directed against the body. More is required of the body now than mere political allegiance or the appropriation of the products of its labor: The new discipline invades the body and seeks to regulate its very forces and operations, the economy and efficiency of its movements.

The disciplinary practices Foucault describes are tied to peculiarly modern forms of the army, the school, the hospital, the prison, and the manufactory; the aim of these disciplines is to increase the utility of the body, to augment its forces:

> What was then being formed was a policy of coercions that act upon the body, a calculated manipulation of its elements, its gestures, its behaviour. The human body was entering a machinery of power that explores it, breaks it down and rearranges it. A 'political anatomy', which was also a 'mechanics of power', was being born; it defined how one may have a hold over others' bodies, not only so that they may do what one wishes, but so that they may operate as one wishes, with the techniques, the speed and the efficiency that one determines. Thus, discipline produces subjected and practiced bodies, 'docile' bodies.[1]

The production of "docile bodies" requires that an uninterrupted coercion be directed to the very processes of bodily activity, not just their result; this "micro-physics of power" fragments and partitions the body's time, its space, and its movements.[2]

modernization of patriarchal domination, a modernization that unfolds historically according to the general pattern described by Foucault.

II

Styles of the female figure vary over time and across cultures: they reflect
cultural obsessions and preoccupations in ways that are still poorly understood.
Today, massiveness, power, or abundance in a woman's body is met with
distaste. The current body of fashion is taut, small-breasted, narrow-hipped,
and of a slimness bordering on emaciation; it is a silhouette that seems more
appropriate to an adolescent boy or a newly pubescent girl than to an adult
woman. Since ordinary women have normally quite different dimensions, they
must of course diet.

Mass-circulation women's magazines run articles on dieting in virtually every
issue. The *Ladies' Home Journal* of February 1986 carries a "Fat-Burning
Exercise Guide," while *Mademoiselle* offers to "Help Stamp Out Cellulite"
with "Six Sleek-Down Strategies." After the diet-busting Christmas holidays
and later, before summer bikini season, the titles of these features become
shriller and more arresting. The reader is now addressed in the imperative
mode: Jump into shape for summer! Shed ugly winter fat with the all-new
Grapefruit Diet! More women than men visit diet doctors, while women greatly
outnumber men in self-help groups such as Weight Watchers and Overeaters
Anonymous—in the case of the latter, by well over 90 percent.[11]

Dieting disciplines the body's hungers: Appetite must be monitored at all
times and governed by an iron will. Since the innocent need of the organism
for food will not be denied, the body becomes one's enemy, an alien being bent
on thwarting the disciplinary project. Anorexia nervosa, which has now assumed epidemic proportions, is to women of the late twentieth century what
hysteria was to women of an earlier day: the crystallization in a pathological
mode of a widespread cultural obsession.[12] A survey taken recently at UCLA
is astounding: Of 260 students interviewed, 27.3 percent of the women but only
5.8 percent of men said they were "terrified" of getting fat: 28.7 percent
of women and only 7.5 percent of men said they were obsessed or "totally
preoccupied" with food. The body images of women and men are strikingly
different as well: 35 percent of women but only 12.5 percent of men said they
felt fat though other people told them they were thin. Women in the survey
wanted to weigh ten pounds less than their average weight; men felt they were
within a pound of their ideal weight. A total of 5.9 percent of women and no
men met the psychiatric criteria for anorexia or bulimia.[13]

Dieting is one discipline imposed upon a body subject to the "tyranny of
slenderness"; exercise is another.[14] Since men as well as women exercise, it is
not always easy in the case of women to distinguish what is done for the
sake of physical fitness from what is done in obedience to the requirements of

femininity. Men as well as women lift weights, do yoga, calisthenics, and aerobics, though "jazzercise" is a largely female pursuit. Men and women alike engage themselves with a variety of machines, each designed to call forth from the body a different exertion: There are Nautilus machines, rowing machines, ordinary and motorized exercycles, portable hip and leg cycles, belt massagers, trampolines; treadmills, arm and leg pulleys. However, given the widespread female obsession with weight, one suspects that many women are working out with these apparatuses in the health club or at the gym with a different aim in mind and in quite a different spirit than the men.

But there are classes of exercises meant for women alone, these designed not to firm or to reduce the body's size overall, but to resculpture its various parts on the current model. M. J. Saffon, "international beauty expert," assures us that his twelve basic facial exercises can erase frown lines, smooth the forehead, raise hollow cheeks, banish crow's feet, and tighten the muscles under the chin.[15] There are exercises to build the breasts and exercises to banish "cellulite," said by "figure consultants" to be a special type of female fat. There is "spot-reducing," an umbrella term that covers dozens of punishing exercises designed to reduce "problem areas" like thick ankles or "saddlebag" thighs. The very idea of "spot-reducing" is both scientifically unsound and cruel, for it raises expectations in women that can never be realized: The pattern in which fat is deposited or removed is known to be genetically determined.

It is not only her natural appetite or unreconstructed contours that pose a danger to women: The very expressions of her face can subvert the disciplinary project of bodily perfection. An expressive face lines and creases more readily than an inexpressive one. Hence, if women are unable to suppress strong emotions, they can at least learn to inhibit the tendency of the face to register them. Sophia Loren recommends a unique solution to this problem: A piece of tape applied to the forehead or between the brows will tug at the skin when one frowns and act as a reminder to relax the face.[16] The tape is to be worn whenever a woman is home alone.

III

There are significant gender differences in gesture, posture, movement, and general bodily comportment: Women are far more restricted than men in their manner of movement and in their lived spatiality. In her classic paper on the subject, Iris Young observes that a space seems to surround women in imagination which they are hesitant to move beyond: This manifests itself both in a reluctance to reach, stretch, and extend the body to meet resistances of matter in motion—as in sport or in the performance of physical tasks—and in a typically constricted posture and general style of movement. Woman's space is not a field in which her bodily intentionality can be freely realized but an enclosure in which she feels herself positioned and by which she is confined.[17] The "loose woman'' violates these norms: Her looseness is manifest not only in her morals, but in her manner of speech, and quite literally in the free and easy way she moves.

In an extraordinary series of over two thousand photographs, many candid shots taken in the street, the German photographer Marianne Wex has documented differences in typical masculine and feminine body posture. Women sit waiting for trains with arms close to the body, hands folded together in their laps, toes pointing straight ahead or turned inward, and legs pressed together.[18] The women in these photographs make themselves small and narrow, harmless; they seem tense; they take up little space. Men, on the other hand, expand into the available space; they sit with legs far apart and arms flung out at some distance from the body. Most common in these sitting male figures is what Wex calls the ''proferring position'': the men sit with legs thrown wide apart, crotch visible, feet pointing outward, often with an arm and casually dangling hand resting comfortably on an open, spread thigh.

In proportion to total body size, a man's stride is longer than a woman's. The man has more spring and rhythm to his step; he walks with toes pointed outward, holds his arms at a greater distance from his body, and swings them farther; he tends to point the whole hand in the direction he is moving. The woman holds her arms closer to her body, palms against her sides; her walk is circumspect. If she has subjected herself to the additional constraint of high-heeled shoes, her body is thrown forward and off-balance: The struggle to walk under these conditions shortens her stride still more.[19]

But women's movement is subjected to a still finer discipline. Feminine faces, as well as bodies, are trained to the expression of deference. Under male scrutiny, women will avert their eyes or cast them downward; the female gaze is trained to abandon its claim to the sovereign status of seer. The ''nice'' girl learns to avoid the bold and unfettered staring of the ''loose'' woman who looks at whatever and whomever she pleases. Women are trained to smile more than men, too. In the economy of smiles, as elsewhere, there is evidence that women are exploited, for they give more than they receive in return; in a smile elicitation study, one researcher found that the rate of smile return by women was 93 percent, by men only 67 percent.[20] In many typical women's jobs, graciousness, deference, and the readiness to serve are part of the work; this requires the worker to fix a smile on her face for a good part of the working day, whatever her inner state.[21] The economy of touching is out of balance, too: men touch women more often and on more parts of the body than women touch men: female secretaries, factory workers, and waitresses report that such liberties are taken routinely with their bodies.[22]

Feminine movement, gesture, and posture must exhibit not only constriction, but grace as well, and a certain eroticism restrained by modesty: all three. Here is field for the operation for a whole new training: A woman must stand with stomach pulled in, shoulders thrown slightly back, and chest out, this to display her bosom to maximum advantage. While she must walk in the confined fashion appropriate to women, her movements must, at the same time, be combined with a subtle but provocative hip-roll. But too much display is taboo: Women in short, low-cut dresses are told to avoid bending over at all, but if they must, great care must be taken to avoid an unseemly display of breast or rump. From time to time, fashion magazines offer quite precise instructions on the proper way of getting in and out of cars. These instructions combine all three imperatives of women's movement: A woman must not allow her arms and legs to flail about in all directions; she must try to manage her movements with the appearance of grace—no small accomplishment when one is climbing out of the back seat of a Fiat—and she is well advised to use the opportunity for a certain display of leg.

All the movements we have described so far are self-movements; they arise from within the woman's own body. But in a way that normally goes unnoticed, males in couples may literally steer a woman everywhere she goes: down the street, around corners, into elevators, through doorways, into her chair at the dinner table, around the dance-floor. The man's movement "is not necessarily heavy and pushy or physical in an ugly way; it is light and gentle but firm in the way of the most confident equestrians with the best trained horses."[23]

IV

We have examined some of the disciplinary practices a woman must master in pursuit of a body of the right size and shape that also displays the proper styles of feminine motility. But woman's body is an ornamented surface too, and there is much discipline involved in this production as well. Here, especially in the application of make-up and the selection of clothes, art and discipline converge, though, as I shall argue, there is less art involved than one might suppose.

A woman's skin must be soft, supple, hairless, and smooth; ideally, it should betray no sign of wear, experience, age, or deep thought. Hair must be removed not only from the face but from large surfaces of the body as well, from legs and thighs, an operation accomplished by shaving, buffing with fine sandpaper, or foul-smelling depilatories. With the new high-leg bathing suits and leotards, a substantial amount of pubic hair must be removed too.[24] The removal of facial hair can be more specialized. Eyebrows are plucked out by the roots with a tweezer. Hot wax is sometimes poured onto the mustache and cheeks and then ripped away when it cools. The woman who wants a more permanent result may try electrolysis: This involves the killing of a hair root by the passage of an electric current down a needle which has been inserted into its base. The procedure is painful and expensive.

The development of what one "beauty expert" calls "good skin-care habits" requires not only attention to health, the avoidance of strong facial expressions,

and the performance of facial exercises, but the regular use of skin-care preparations, many to be applied oftener than once a day: cleansing lotions (ordinary
soap and water "upsets the skin's acid and alkaline balance"), wash-off cleans-
ers (milder than cleansing lotions), astringents, toners, make-up removers, night
creams, nourishing creams, eye creams, moisturizers, skin balancers, body
lotions, hand creams, lip pomades, suntan lotions, sun screens, facial masks.
Provision of the proper facial mask is complex: There are sulfur masks for
pimples; hot or oil masks for dry areas; also cold masks for dry areas; tightening
masks; conditioning masks; peeling masks; cleansing masks made of herbs,
cornmeal, or almonds; mud packs. Black women may wish to use "fade
creams" to "even skin tone." Skin-care preparations are never just sloshed
onto the skin, but applied according to precise rules: Eye cream is dabbed on
gently in movements toward, never away from, the nose; cleansing cream is
applied in outward directions only, straight across the forehead, the upper lip,
and the chin, never up but straight down the nose and up and out on the
cheeks.[25]

The normalizing discourse of modern medicine is enlisted by the cosmetics
industry to gain credibility for its claims. Dr. Christiaan Barnard lends his
enormous prestige to the Glycel line of "cellular treatment activators"; these
contain "glycosphingolipids" that can "make older skin behave and look like
younger skin." The Clinique computer at any Clinique counter will select a
combination of preparations just right for you. Ultima II contains "procollagen"
in its anti-aging eye cream that "provides hydration" to "demoralizing lines."
"Biotherm" eye cream dramatically improves the "biomechanical properties
of the skin."[26] The Park Avenue clinic of Dr. Zizmor, "chief of dermatology
at one of New York's leading hospitals," offers not only medical treatment
such as dermabrasion and chemical peeling but "total deep skin cleansing" as
well.[27]

Really good skin-care habits require the use of a variety of aids and devices:
facial steamers; faucet filters to collect impurities in the water; borax to soften
it; a humidifier for the bedroom; electric massagers; backbrushes; complexion
brushes; loofahs; pumice stones; blackhead removers. I will not detail the imple-
ments or techniques involved in the manicure or pedicure.

The ordinary circumstances of life as well as a wide variety of activities cause
a crisis in skin-care and require a stepping up of the regimen as well as an
additional laying on of preparations. Skin-care discipline requires a specialized
knowledge: A woman must know what to do if she has been skiing, taking
medication, doing vigorous exercise, boating, or swimming in chlorinated
pools; if she has been exposed to pollution, heated rooms, cold, sun, harsh
weather, the pressurized cabins on airplanes, saunas or steam rooms, fatigue
or stress. Like the schoolchild or prisoner, the woman mastering good skin-
care habits is put on a timetable: Georgette Klinger requires that a shorter or
longer period of attention be paid to the complexion at least four times a day.[28]

Hair-care, like skin-care, requires a similar investment of time, the use of a wide variety of preparations, the mastery of a set of techniques and again, the acquisition of a specialized knowledge.

The crown and pinnacle of good hair care and skin care is, of course, the arrangement of the hair and the application of cosmetics. Here the regimen of hair care, skin care, manicure, and pedicure is recapitulated in another mode. A woman must learn the proper manipulation of a large number of devices—the blow dryer, styling brush, curling iron, hot curlers, wire curlers, eye-liner, lipliner, lipstick brush, eyelash curler, mascara brush—and the correct manner of application of a wide variety of products—foundation, toner, covering stick, mascara, eye shadow, eye gloss, blusher, lipstick, rouge, lip gloss, hair dye, hair rinse, hair lightener, hair "relaxer," etc.

In the language of fashion magazines and cosmetic ads, making up is typically portrayed as an aesthetic activity in which a woman can express her individuality. In reality, while cosmetic styles change every decade or so and while some variation in make-up is permitted depending on the occasion, making up the face is, in fact, a highly stylized activity that gives little rein to self-expression. Painting the face is not like painting a picture; at best, it might be described as painting the same picture over and over again with minor variations. Little latitude is permitted in what is considered appropriate make-up for the office and for most social occasions; indeed, the woman who uses cosmetics in a genuinely novel and imaginative way is liable to be seen not as an artist but as an eccentric. Furthermore, since a properly made-up face is, if not a card of entrée, at least a badge of acceptability in most social and professional contexts, the woman who chooses not to wear cosmetics at all faces sanctions of a sort which will never be applied to someone who chooses not to paint a watercolor.

V

Are we dealing in all this merely with sexual *difference?* Scarcely. The disciplinary practices I have described are part of the process by which the ideal body of femininity—and hence the feminine body-subject—is constructed; in doing this, they produce a "practiced and subjected" body, i.e., a body on which an inferior status has been inscribed. A woman's face must be made up, that is to say, made over, and so must her body: she is ten pounds overweight; her lips must be made more kissable; her complexion dewier; her eyes more mysterious. The "art" of make-up is the art of disguise, but this presupposes that a woman's face, unpainted, is defective. Soap and water, a shave, and routine attention to hygiene may be enough for *him;* for *her* they are not. The strategy of much beauty-related advertising is to suggest to women that their bodies are deficient, but even without such more or less explicit teaching, the media images of perfect female beauty which bombard us daily leave no doubt in the minds of most women that they fail to measure up. The technologies of femininity are taken up and practiced by women against the background of a pervasive sense of bodily deficiency: This accounts for what is often their compulsive or even ritualistic character.

The disciplinary project of femininity is a "set-up": It requires such radical and extensive measures of bodily transformation that virtually every woman who gives herself to it is destined in some degree to fail. Thus, a measure of shame is added to a woman's sense that the body she inhabits is deficient: she ought to take better care of herself; she might after all have jogged that last mile. Many women are without the time or resources to provide themselves with even the minimum of what such a regimen requires, e.g., a decent diet. Here is an additional source of shame for poor women who must bear what our society regards as the more general shame of poverty. The burdens poor women bear in this regard are not merely psychological, since conformity to the prevailing standards of bodily acceptability is a known factor in economic mobility.

The larger disciplines that construct a "feminine" body out of a female one are by no means race- or class-specific. There is little evidence that women of color or working-class women are in general less committed to the incarnation of an ideal femininity than their more privileged sisters. This is not to deny the many ways in which factors of race, class, locality, ethnicity, or personal taste can be expressed within the kinds of practices I have described. The rising young corporate executive may buy her cosmetics at Bergdorf-Goodman while the counter-server at McDonald's gets hers at the K-Mart; the one may join an expensive "upscale" health club, while the other may have to make do with the $9.49 GFX Body-Flex II Home-Gym advertised in the *National Enquirer:* Both are aiming at the same general result.[29]

In the regime of institutionalized heterosexuality woman must make herself "object and prey" for the man: It is for him that these eyes are limpid pools, this cheek baby-smooth.[30] In contemporary patriarchal culture, a panoptical male connoisseur resides within the consciousness of most women: They stand perpetually before his gaze and under his judgment. Woman lives her body as seen by another, by an anonymous patriarchal Other. We are often told that "women dress for other women." There is some truth in this: Who but someone engaged in a project similar to my own can appreciate the panache with which I bring it off? But women know for whom this game is played: They know that a pretty young woman is likelier to become a flight attendant than a plain one and that a well-preserved older woman has a better chance of holding onto her husband than one who has "let herself go."

Here it might be objected that performance for another in no way signals the inferiority of the performer to the one for whom the performance is intended: The actor, for example, depends on his audience but is in no way inferior to it; he is not demeaned by his dependency. While femininity is surely something enacted, the analogy to theater breaks down in a number of ways. First, as I argued earlier, the self-determination we think of as requisite to an artistic career is lacking here: Femininity as spectacle is something in which virtually every woman is required to participate. Second, the precise nature of the criteria by which women are judged, not only the inescapability of judgment itself, reflects gross imbalances in the social power of the sexes that do not mark the relationship of artists and their audiences. An aesthetic of femininity, for example, that mandates fragility and a lack of muscular strength produces female bodies that can offer little resistance to physical abuse, and the physical abuse of women by men, as we know, is widespread. It is true that the current fitness movement has permitted women to develop more muscular strength and endurance than was heretofore allowed; indeed, images of women have begun to appear in the mass media that seem to eroticize this new muscularity. But a woman may by no means develop more muscular strength than her partner; the bride who would tenderly carry her groom across the threshold is a figure of comedy, not romance.[31]

Under the current "tyranny of slenderness" women are forbidden to become large or massive; they must take up as little space as possible. The very contours a woman's body takes on as she matures—the fuller breasts and rounded hips— have become distasteful. The body by which a woman feels herself judged and which by rigorous discipline she must try to assume is the body of early adolescence, slight and unformed, a body lacking flesh or substance, a body in whose very contours the image of immaturity has been inscribed. The requirement that a woman maintain a smooth and hairless skin carries further the theme of inexperience, for an infantilized face must accompany her infantilized body, a face that never ages or furrows its brow in thought. The face of the ideally feminine woman must never display the marks of character, wisdom, and experience that we so admire in men.

To succeed in the provision of a beautiful or sexy body gains a woman attention and some admiration but little real respect and rarely any social power. A woman's effort to master feminine body discipline will lack importance just because she does it: Her activity partakes of the general depreciation of everything female. In spite of unrelenting pressure to "make the most of what they have," women are ridiculed and dismissed for the triviality of their interest in such "trivial" things as clothes and make-up. Further, the narrow identification of woman with sexuality and the body in a society that has for centuries displayed profound suspicion toward both does little to raise her status. Even the most adored female bodies complain routinely of their situation in ways that reveal an implicit understanding that there is something demeaning in the kind of attention they receive. Marilyn Monroe, Elizabeth Taylor, and Farrah Fawcett have all wanted passionately to become actresses-artists and not just "sex objects."

But it is perhaps in their more restricted motility and comportment that the inferiorization of women's bodies is most evident: Women's typical body language, a language of relative tension and constriction, is understood to be a language of subordination when it is enacted by men in male status hierarchies. In groups of men, those with higher status typically assume looser and more relaxed postures: The boss lounges comfortably behind the desk while the applicant sits tense and rigid on the edge of his seat. Higher-status individuals may touch their subordinates more than they themselves get touched; they initiate more eye contact and are smiled at by their inferiors more than they are observed to smile in return.[32] What is announced in the comportment of superiors is confidence and ease, especially ease of access to the Other. Female constraint in posture and movement is no doubt over-determined: The fact that women tend to sit and stand with legs, feet, and knees close or touching may well be a coded declaration of sexual circumspection in a society that still maintains a double standard, or an effort, albeit unconscious, to guard the genital area. In the latter case, a woman's tight and constricted posture must be seen as the expression of her need to ward off real or symbolic sexual attack. Whatever proportions must be assigned in the final display to fear or deference, one thing is clear: Woman's body language speaks eloquently, though silently, of her subordinate status in a hierarchy of gender.

VI

If what we have described is a genuine discipline—a "system of micro-power that is essentially non-egalitarian and asymetrical"—who then are the disciplinarians?[33] Who is the top sergeant in the disciplinary regime of femininity? Historically, the law has had some responsibility for enforcement: In times gone by, for example, individuals who appeared in public in the clothes of the other sex could be arrested. While cross-dressers are still liable to some harassment, the kind of discipline we are considering is not the business of the police or the courts. Parents and teachers, of course, have extensive influence, admonishing girls to be demure and ladylike, to "smile pretty," to sit with their legs together. The influence of the media is pervasive, too, constructing as it does an image of the female body as spectacle, nor can we ignore the role played by "beauty experts" or by emblematic public personages such as Jane Fonda and Lynn Redgrave.

But none of these individuals—the skin-care consultant, the parent, the policeman—does in fact wield the kind of authority that is typically invested in those who manage more straightforward disciplinary institutions. The disciplinary power that inscribes femininity in the female body is everywhere and it is nowhere; the disciplinarian is everyone and yet no one in particular. Women regarded as overweight, for example, report that they are regularly admonished to diet, sometimes by people they scarcely know. These intrusions are often softened by reference to the natural prettiness just waiting to emerge: "People have always said that I had a beautiful face and 'if you'd only lose weight you'd be really beautiful.' ''[34] Here, "people"—friends and casual acquaintances alike—act to enforce prevailing standards of body size.

Foucault tends to identify the imposition of discipline upon the body with the operation of specific institutions, e.g., the school, the factory, the prison. To do this, however, is to overlook the extent to which discipline can be institutionally *unbound* as well as institutionally bound.[35] The anonymity of disciplinary power and its wide dispersion have consequences which are crucial to a proper understanding of the subordination of women. The absence of a formal institutional structure and of authorities invested with the power to carry out institutional directives creates the impression that the production of femininity is either entirely voluntary or natural. The several senses of "discipline" are instructive here. On the one hand, discipline is something imposed on subjects of an "essentially inegalitarian and asymetrical" system of authority. Schoolchildren, convicts, and draftees are subject to discipline in this sense. But discipline can be sought voluntarily as well, as, for example, when an individual seeks initiation into the spiritual discipline of Zen Buddhism. Discipline can, of course, be both at once: The volunteer may seek the physical and occupational training offered by the army without the army's ceasing in any way to be the instrument by which he and other members of his class are kept in disciplined subjection. Feminine bodily discipline has this dual character: On the one hand, no one is marched off for electrolysis at the end of a rifle, nor can we fail to appreciate the initiative and ingenuity displayed by countless women in an attempt to master the rituals of beauty. Nevertheless, insofar as the disciplinary practices of femininity produce a "subjected and practiced," an inferiorized, body, they must be understood as aspects of a far larger discipline, an oppressive and inegalitarian system of sexual subordination. This system aims at turning women into the docile and compliant companions of men just as surely as the army aims to turn its raw recruits into soldiers.

Now the transformation of oneself into a properly feminine body may be any or all of the following: a rite of passage into adulthood; the adoption and celebration of a particular aesthetic; a way of announcing one's economic level and social status; a way to triumph over other women in the competition for men or jobs; or an opportunity for massive narcissistic indulgence.[36] The social construction of the feminine body is all these things, but it is at base discipline, too, and discipline of the inegalitarian sort. The absence of formally identifiable disciplinarians and of a public schedule of sanctions serves only to disguise the extent to which the imperative to be "feminine" serves the interest of domination. This is a lie in which all concur: Making up is merely artful play; one's first pair of high-heeled shoes is an innocent part of growing up and not the modern equivalent of foot-binding.

Why aren't all women feminists? In modern industrial societies, women are not kept in line by fear of retaliatory male violence; their victimization is not that of the South African black. Nor will it suffice to say that a false consciousness engendered in women by patriarchal ideology is at the basis of female subordination. This is not to deny the fact that women are often subject to gross male violence or that women and men alike are ideologically mystified by the dominant gender arrangements. What I wish to suggest instead is that an adequate understanding of women's oppression will require an appreciation of the extent to which not only women's lives but their very subjectivities are structured within an ensemble of systematically duplicitous practices. The feminine discipline of the body is a case in point: The practices which construct this body have an overt aim and character far removed, indeed radically distinct, from their covert function. In this regard, the system of gender subordination, like the wage-bargain under capitalism, illustrates in its own way the ancient tension between what is and what appears: The phenomenal forms in which it is manifested are often quite different from the real relations which form its deeper structure.

VII

The lack of formal public sanctions does not mean that a woman who is unable or unwilling to submit herself to the appropriate body discipline will face no sanctions at all. On the contrary, she faces a very severe sanction indeed in a world dominated by men: the refusal of male patronage. For the heterosexual woman, this may mean the loss of a badly needed intimacy; for both heterosexual women and lesbians, it may well mean the refusal of a decent livelihood.

As noted earlier, women punish themselves too for the failure to conform. The growing literature on women's body size is filled with wrenching confessions of shame from the overweight:

> I felt clumsy and huge. I felt that I would knock over furniture, bump into things, tip over chairs, not fit into VW's, especially when people were trying to crowd into the back seat. I felt like I was taking over the whole room. . . . I felt disgusting and like a slob. In the summer I felt hot and sweaty and I knew people saw my sweat as evidence that I was too fat.

> I feel so terrible about the way I look that I cut off connection with my body. I operate from the neck up. I do not look in mirrors. I do not want to spend time buying clothes. I do not want to spend time with make-up because its painful for me to look at myself.[37]

> I can no longer bear to look at myself. Whenever I have to stand in front of a mirror to comb my hair I tie a large towel around my neck. Even at night I slip my nightgown on before I take off my blouse and pants. But all this has only made it worse and worse. It's been so long since I've really looked at my body.[38]

The depth of these women's shame is a measure of the extent to which all women have internalized patriarchal standards of bodily acceptability. A fuller examination of what is meant here by "internalization" may shed light on a question posed earlier: Why isn't every woman a feminist?

Something is "internalized" when it gets incorporated into the structure of the self. By "structure of the self" I refer to those modes of perception and of self-perception which allow a self to distinguish itself both from other selves and from things which are not selves. I have described elsewhere how a generalized male witness comes to structure woman's consciousness of herself as a bodily being.[39] This, then, is one meaning of "internalization." The sense of oneself as a distinct and valuable individual is tied not only to the sense of how one is perceived, but also to what one knows, especially to what one knows how to do; this is a second sense of "internalization." Whatever its ultimate effect, discipline can provide the individual upon whom it is imposed with a sense of mastery as well as a secure sense of identity. There is a certain contradiction here: While its imposition may promote a larger disempowerment, discipline may bring with it a certain development of a person's powers. Women, then, like other skilled individuals, have a stake in the perpetuation of their skills, whatever it may have cost to acquire them and quite apart from the question whether, as a gender, they would have been better off had they never had to acquire them in the first place. Hence, feminism, especially a genuinely radical feminism that questions the patriarchal construction of the female body, threatens women with a certain de-skilling, something people normally resist: Beyond this, it calls into question that aspect of personal identity which is tied to the development of a sense of competence.

Resistance from this source may be joined by a reluctance to part with the rewards of compliance; further, many women will resist the abandonment of an aesthetic that defines what they take to be beautiful. But there is still another source of resistance, one more subtle perhaps, but tied once again to questions of identity and internalization. To have a body felt to be "feminine"—a body socially constructed through the appropriate practices—is in most cases crucial to a woman's sense of herself as female and, since persons currently can *be* only as male or female, to her sense of herself as an existing individual. To possess such a body may also be essential to her sense of herself as a sexually desiring and desirable subject. Hence, any political project which aims to dismantle the machinery that turns a female body into a feminine one may well be apprehended by a woman as something that threatens her with desexualization, if not outright annihilation.

The categories of masculinity and femininity do more than assist in the construction of personal identities; they are critical elements in our informal social ontology. This may account to some degree for the otherwise puzzling phenomenon of homophobia and for the revulsion felt by many at the sight of female bodybuilders; neither the homosexual nor the muscular woman can be assimilated easily into the categories that structure everyday life. The radical feminist critique of femininity, then, may pose a threat not only to a woman's sense of her own identity and desirability but to the very structure of her social universe.

Of course, many women *are* feminists, favoring a program of political and economic reform in the struggle to gain equality with men.[40] But many "reform" or liberal feminists, indeed, many orthodox Marxists, are committed to the idea that the preservation of a woman's femininity is quite compatible with her struggle for liberation.[41] These thinkers have rejected a normative femininity based upon the notion of "separate spheres" and the traditional sexual division of labor while accepting at the same time conventional standards of feminine body display. If my analysis is correct, such a feminism is incoherent. Foucault has argued that modern bourgeois democracy is deeply flawed in that it seeks political rights for individuals constituted as unfree by a variety of disciplinary micropowers that lie beyond the realm of what is ordinarily defined as the "political." "The man described for us whom we are invited to free," he says, "is already in himself the effect of a subjection much more profound than himself."[42] If, as I have argued, female subjectivity is constituted in any significant measure in and through the disciplinary practices that construct the feminine body, what Foucault says here of "man" is perhaps even truer of "woman." Marxists have maintained from the first the inadequacy of a purely liberal feminism: We have reached the same conclusion through a different route, casting doubt at the same time on the adequacy of traditional Marxist prescriptions for women's liberation as well. Liberals call for equal rights for women, traditional Marxists for the entry of women into production on an equal footing with men, the socialization of housework and proletarian revolution; neither calls for the deconstruction of the categories of masculinity and femininity.[43] Femininity as a certain "style of the flesh" will have to be surpassed in the direction of something quite different, not masculinity, which is in many ways only its mirror opposite, but a radical and as yet unimagined transformation of the female body.

VIII

Foucault has argued that the transition from traditional to modern societies has been characterized by a profound transformation in the exercise of power, by what he calls "a reversal of the political axis of individualization."[44] In older authoritarian systems, power was embodied in the person of the monarch and exercised upon a largely anonymous body of subjects; violation of the law was seen as an insult to the royal individual. While the methods employed to enforce compliance in the past were often quite brutal, involving gross assaults against the body, power in such a system operated in a haphazard and discontinuous fashion; much in the social totality lay beyond its reach.

By contrast, modern society has seen the emergence of increasingly invasive apparatuses of power: These exercise a far more restrictive social and psychological control than was heretofore possible. In modern societies, effects of power "circulate through progressively finer channels, gaining access to individuals themselves, to their bodies, their gestures and all their daily actions."[45] Power now seeks to transform the minds of those individuals who might be tempted to resist it, not merely to punish or imprison their bodies. This requires two things: a finer control of the body's time and its movements—a control that cannot be achieved without ceaseless surveillance and a better understanding of the specific person, of the genesis and nature of his "case." The power these new apparatuses seek to exercise requires a new knowledge of the individual: Modern psychology and sociology are born. Whether the new modes of control have charge of correction, production, education, or the provision of welfare, they resemble one another; they exercise power in a bureaucratic mode—faceless, centralized, and pervasive. A reversal has occurred: Power has now become anonymous, while the project of control has brought into being a new individuality. In fact, Foucault believes that the operation of power constitutes the very subjectivity of the subject. Here, the image of the Panopticon returns: Knowing that he may be observed from the tower at any time, the inmate takes over the job of policing himself. The gaze which is inscribed in the very structure of the disciplinary institution is internalized by the inmate: Modern technologies of behavior are thus oriented toward the production of isolated and self-policing subjects.[46]

Women have their own experience of the modernization of power, one which begins later but follows in many respects the course outlined by Foucault. In important ways, a woman's behavior is less regulated now than it was in the past. She has more mobility and is less confined to domestic space. She enjoys what to previous generations would have been an unimaginable sexual liberty. Divorce, access to paid work outside the home, and the increasing secularization of modern life have loosened the hold over her of the traditional family and, in spite of the current fundamentalist revival, of the church. Power in these institutions was wielded by individuals known to her. Husbands and fathers enforced patriarchal authority in the family. As in the *ancien régime,* a woman's body was subject to sanctions if she disobeyed. Not Foucault's royal individual but the Divine Individual decreed that her desire be always "unto her husband," while the person of the priest made known to her God's more specific intentions concerning her place and duties. In the days when civil and ecclesiastical authority were still conjoined, individuals formally invested with power were charged with the correction of recalcitrant women whom the family had somehow failed to constrain.

By contrast, the disciplinary power that is increasingly charged with the production of a properly embodied femininity is dispersed and anonymous; there are no individuals formally empowered to wield it; it is, as we have seen, invested in everyone and in no one in particular. This disciplinary power is peculiarly modern: It does not rely upon violent or public sanctions, nor does it seek to restrain the freedom of the female body to move from place to place. For all that, its invasion of the body is well-nigh total: The female body enters "a machinery of power that explores it, breaks it down and rearranges it."[47] The disciplinary techniques through which the "docile bodies" of women are constructed aim at a regulation which is perpetual and exhaustive—a regulation of the body's size and contours, its appetite, posture, gestures, and general comportment in space and the appearance of each of its visible parts.

As modern industrial societies change and as women themselves offer resistance to patriarchy, older forms of domination are eroded. But new forms arise, spread, and become consolidated. Women are no longer required to be chaste or modest, to restrict their sphere of activity to the home, or even to realize their properly feminine destiny in maternity: Normative femininity is coming more and more to be centered on woman's body—not its duties and obligations or even its capacity to bear children, but its sexuality, more precisely, its presumed heterosexuality and its appearance. There is, of course, nothing new in women's preoccupation with youth and beauty. What is new is the growing power of the image in a society increasingly oriented toward the visual media. Images of normative femininity, it might be ventured, have replaced the religiously oriented tracts of the past. New too is the spread of this discipline to all classes of women and its deployment throughout the life-cycle. What was formerly the speciality of the aristocrat or courtesan is now the routine obligation of every woman, be she a grandmother or a barely pubescent girl.

To subject oneself to the new disciplinary power is to be up-to-date, to be "with-it"; as I have argued, it is presented to us in ways that are regularly disguised. It is fully compatible with the current need for women's wage labor, the cult of youth and fitness, and the need of advanced capitalism to maintain high levels of consumption. Further, it represents a saving in the economy of enforcement: Since it is women themselves who practice this discipline on and against their own bodies, men get off scot-free.

The woman who checks her make-up half a dozen times a day to see if her foundation has caked or her mascara run, who worries that the wind or rain may spoil her hairdo, who looks frequently to see if her stockings have bagged at the ankle, or who, feeling fat, monitors everything she eats, has become, just as surely as the inmate of Panopticon, a self-policing subject, a self committed to a relentless self-surveillance. This self-surveillance is a form of obedience to patriarchy. It is also the reflection in woman's consciousness of the fact that *she* is under surveillance in ways that *he* is not, that whatever else she may become, she is importantly a body designed to please or to excite. There has been induced in many women, then, in Foucault's words, "a state of conscious and permanent visibility that assures the automatic functioning of power."[48] Since the standards of female bodily acceptability are impossible fully to realize, requiring as they do a virtual transcendence of nature, a woman may live much of her life with a pervasive feeling of bodily deficiency. Hence, a tighter control of the body has gained a new kind of hold over the mind.

Foucault often writes as if power constitutes the very individuals upon whom it operates:

> The individual is not to be conceived as a sort of elementary nucleus, a primitive atom, a multiple and inert material on which power comes to fasten or against which it happens to strike. . . . In fact, it is already one of the prime effects of power that certain bodies, certain gestures, certain discourses, certain desires, come to be identified and constituted as individuals.[49]

Nevertheless, if individuals were wholly constituted by the power/knowledge regime Foucault describes, it would make no sense to speak of resistance to discipline at all. Foucault seems sometimes on the verge of depriving us of a vocabulary in which to conceptualize the nature and meaning of those periodic refusals of control which, just as much as the imposition of control, mark the course of human history.

Peter Dews accuses Foucault of lacking a theory of the "libidinal body," i.e., the body upon which discipline is imposed and whose bedrock impulse toward spontaneity and pleasure might perhaps become the locus of resistance.[50] Do women's "libidinal" bodies, then, not rebel against the pain, constriction, tedium, semi-starvation, and constant self-surveillance to which they are currently condemned? Certainly they do, but the rebellion is put down every time a woman picks up her eyebrow tweezers or embarks upon a new diet. The harshness of a regimen alone does not guarantee its rejection, for hardships can be endured if they are thought to be necessary or inevitable.

While "nature," in the form of a "libidinal" body, may not be the origin of a revolt against "culture," domination and the discipline it requires are never imposed without some cost. Historically, the forms and occasions of resistance are manifold. Sometimes, instances of resistance appear to spring from the introduction of new and conflicting factors into the lives of the dominated: The juxtaposition of old and new and the resulting incoherence or "contradiction" may make submission to the old ways seem increasingly unnecessary. In the present instance, what may be a major factor in the relentless and escalating objectification of women's bodies—namely, women's growing independence—produces in many women a sense of incoherence that calls into question the meaning and necessity of the current discipline. As women (albeit a small minority of women) begin to realize an unprecedented political, economic, and sexual self-determination, they fall ever more completely under the dominating gaze of patriarchy. It is this paradox, not the "libidinal body," that produces, here and there, pockets of resistance.

In the current political climate, there is no reason to anticipate either widespread resistance to currently fashionable modes of feminine embodiment or joyous experimentation with new "styles of the flesh"; moreover, such novelties would face profound opposition from material and psychological sources identified earlier in this essay (see Section VII). In spite of this, a number of oppositional discourses and practices have appeared in recent years. An increasing number of women are "pumping iron," a few with little concern for the limits of body development imposed by current canons of femininity. Women in radical lesbian communities have also rejected hegemonic images of femininity and are struggling to develop a new female aesthetic. A striking feature of such communities is the extent to which they have overcome the oppressive identification of female beauty and desirability with youth: Here, the physical features of aging—"character" lines and greying hair—not only do not diminish a woman's attractiveness, they may even enhance it. A popular literature of resistance is growing, some of it analytical and reflective, like Kim Chernin's *The Obsession,* some oriented toward practical self-help, like Marcia Hutchinson's recent *Transforming Body Image: Learning to Love the Body You Have.*[51] This literature reflects a mood akin in some ways to that other and earlier mood of quiet desperation to which Betty Friedan gave voice in *The Feminine Mystique.* Nor should we forget that a mass-based women's movement is in place in this country which has begun a critical questioning of the meaning of femininity, if not yet in this, then in other domains of life. We women cannot begin the re-vision of our own bodies until we learn to read the cultural messages we inscribe upon them daily and until we come to see that even when the mastery of the disciplines of femininity produce a triumphant result, we are still only women.

6

Shame and Gender

Contemporary philosophers have largely abandoned an older philosophical psychology which distinguished sharply between reason and emotion and which regarded feeling as no more able than imagination or desire to determine the real nature of things. By contrast, the inextricability of cognition and emotion is now widely recognized. A number of Anglo-American philosophers have argued that our emotions presuppose beliefs and can therefore be evaluated for their rationality,[1] while in a similar vein, existential philosophers, have maintained that affective states have a cognitive dimension in that they may be disclosive of a subject's "Being-in-the-world." Heidegger, for example, has claimed that every human being (*Dasein*) has, *a priori*, necessary features of existence, among which are understanding (*Verstehen*) and state-of-mind (*Befindlichkeit*). The latter—literally, "the state in which one may be found" (from *sich befinden*, "to find oneself")—refers both to the finding *that* one is situated in a world and to the particular *how* of this situation; this "finding" can occur only insofar as *Dasein* has moods, feelings, or humours that constitute its openness or "attunement" (*Gestimmtheit*) to Being. "A mood makes manifest 'how one is and how one is faring' "; boredom, joy, and above all dread are ontologically disclosive in ways that a passionless pure beholding can never be.[2] These and other states of mind constitute a primordial disclosure of self and world whereby "we can encounter something that matters to us": Indeed, insofar as emotional attunement is held to be an *a priori*, necessary feature of any possible human existence, it follows that pure acts of cognition are themselves impossible and that knowing will have its own affective taste.[3]

Women are situated differently than men within the ensemble of social relations. For this reason, feminist philosophers have argued that women's ways of knowing are different than men's, that both the specific character of the world's disclosure as well as the modes of this disclosure are in some, though not in all important ways gender-specific and that the abstract, purportedly genderless epistemic subject of traditional philosophy is really a male subject in disguise.[4] Now if knowing cannot be described in ways that are gender-neutral, neither can feeling. Differences between men and women are most often described in the language of character traits or dispositions: It is often said of women, for example, that they are less assertive than men, more preoc-cupied with their appearance, etc. But what is not captured by the language of disposition is the affective taste of a low level of assertion or a sense of the larger emotional constellation in which a feminine preoccupation with appearance is situated.

A number of recent empirical studies have confirmed what common observa-tion has reported all along, namely, that the feeling lives of men and women are not identical.[5] But what needs to be asked about such emotional differences is not only their relationship to typical gendered traits or dispositions but, fol-lowing Heidegger, the way in which such attunements are disclosive of their subjects' "Being-in-the-world," i.e., of their character as selves and of the specific ways in which, as selves, they are inscribed within the social totality. The search for a feminist reconstruction of knowledge, then, must be augmented by a study of the most pervasive patterns of gendered emotion in their revelatory moment. Insofar as women are not just situated differently than men within the social ensemble, but are actively subordinated to them within it, this project—the identification and description of these attunements—will be at the same time a contribution to the phenomenology of oppression.

What patterns of mood or feeling, then, tend to characterize women more than men? Here are some candidates: shame; guilt; the peculiar dialectic of shame and pride in embodiment consequent upon a narcissistic assumption of the body as spectacle; the blissful loss of self in the sense of merger with another; the pervasive apprehension consequent upon physical vulnerability, especially the fear of rape or assault. Since I have no doubt that men and women have the same fundamental emotional capacities, to say that some pattern of feeling in women, say shame, is gender-related is not to claim that it is gender-specific, i.e., that men are never ashamed; it is only to claim that women are more prone to experience the emotion in question and that the feeling itself has a different meaning in relation to their total psychic situation and general social location than has a similar emotion when experienced by men. Some of the commoner forms of shame in men, for example, may be intelligible only in light of the presupposition of male power, while in women shame may well be a mark and token of powerlessness. We recognize in everyday speech the prone-ness of certain classes of persons to particular patterns of feeling: It is often said of ghetto blacks, for example, that they have feelings of hopelessness and that they are depressed and despairing. This is not to say that rich white people never despair or feel depressed, only that members of the "underclass" are more given to feelings of hopelessness than more privileged people and that the despair they feel is peculiarly disclosive of the realities of their lives.

In what follows, I shall examine women's shame, not the alteration of pride and shame called forth by the imperatives of feminine body display, nor the shame of women who feel that they are fat, old or ugly. (But see of course Chapters 3 and 5 above.) The shame I want to pursue now is less specific; its boundaries are blurred; it is less available to consciousness and more likely to be denied. This shame is manifest in a pervasive sense of personal inadequacy that, like the shame of embodiment, is profoundly disempowering; both reveal the "generalized condition of dishonor" which is woman's lot in sexist society.[6] I shall maintain that women typically are more shame-prone than men, that shame is not so much a particular feeling or emotion (though it involves specific feelings and emotions) as a pervasive affective attunement to the social environment, that women's shame is more than merely an effect of subordination but, within the larger universe of patriarchal social relations, a profound mode of disclosure both of self and situation. I shall argue, too, that moral psychology as currently practiced fails to do justice to the quite common kind of shame I shall be at some pains to describe. Finally, I shall offer a diagnosis of this failure.

II

Shame can be characterized in a preliminary way as a species of psychic distress occasioned by a self or a state of the self apprehended as inferior, defective, or in some way diminished.[7] For the Sartre of *Being and Nothingness,* shame requires an audience: shame is "in its primary structure shame *before somebody*": it is "shame *of oneself* before the Other."[8] "Nobody," he says, "can be vulgar all alone"![9] To be ashamed is to be in the position of "passing judgment on myself as on an object, for it is as an object that I appear to the Other."[10] Only insofar as I apprehend myself as the Other's object, i.e., through the medium of another consciousness, can I grasp my own object-character. Hence, shame before the Other is primordial: I must feel shame before some actual Other before I learn to raise an internalized Other in imagination. Furthermore, "shame is by nature recognition": Unless I recognize that I *am* as I am seen by the Other, the Other's judgment cannot cast me down.[11]

Sartre's discussion of shame is highly abbreviated: Preoccupied with the role of the Other as audience, he has little to say about the mechanisms that can forge an identification of self and Other in an experience of shame. Once an actual Other has revealed my object-character to me, I can become an object for myself; I can come to see myself as I might be seen by another, caught in the shameful act. Hence, I *can* succeed in being vulgar all alone: In such a situation, the Other before whom I am ashamed is only—myself. "A man may feel himself disgraced,'' says Isenberg, ''by something that is unworthy in his own eyes and apart from any judgment but his own.''[12]

Here is a fuller characterization of the structure of shame: Shame is the distressed apprehension of the self as inadequate or diminished: it requires if not an actual audience before whom my deficiencies are paraded, then an internalized audience with the capacity to judge me, hence internalized standards of judgment. Further, shame requires the recognition that I *am,* in some important sense, as I am seen to be.

Gabriele Taylor takes issue with the Sartrian idea—an idea I endorse—that ''recognition'' is a feature of every shame experience. She takes Sartre to mean that the distress involved in feeling ashamed is called forth only insofar as I myself identify with the values and perspective of the one whose gaze has shamed me. She sets against this claim a number of counterexamples, the most interesting drawn from Scheler: An artist's model feels shame when she realizes that the artist, with whom she thought she had a purely business relationship, has come to regard her with desire. In this case, the model ''need not see herself as a woman in the sense of 'object of sexual interest' . . . she does not identify with the audience, she sees rather how she appears to the artist.''[13] But surely, what I *am,* that is, what I am made to be—here, a desirable body—is not always up to me to determine: Here, how I am and how I appear to the other converge. The model's evidence that she *is* as she is seen to be lies just in the desiring gaze of the artist. The identificatory recognition of herself in the artist's eye has not been chosen, nor is it welcome, nor does it coincide with the idea of herself she would like him to have of her, but it is recognition nevertheless. The model falls from innocence in this play of eyes: She has no choice but to see herself as an ''object of sexual interest.''

Like Sartre, John Deigh underscores the intersubjective structure of shame. We should ''conceive shame, not as a reaction to a loss, but as a reaction to a threat, specifically the threat of demeaning treatment one would invite in giving the appearance of someone of lesser worth.''[14] But this seems excessively narrow. Surely, shame is sometimes a reaction to real loss, to loss of face, this occasioned by the disclosure to oneself or to others of defects in the self that may come suddenly and horribly to light. At any rate, Deigh's definition bears clearly upon additional aspects of the shame experience: the cringing withdrawal from others; the cringing within, this felt sometimes as a physical sensation of being pulled inward and downward; the necessity for hiding and concealment. All are typical responses to threat. The painful disclosure of one's shortcomings, actual or feared, may lead to ''a shattering of trust in oneself, even in one's own body and skill and identity,'' and, since whatever is found shameful in oneself may reflect the character of one's normal social network, ''in the trusted boundaries or framework of the society and the world one has known.''[15] Hence, ''shame, an experience of violation of trust in oneself and in the world, may go deeper than guilt for a specific act.''[16]

Deigh takes issue with John Rawls's account of shame in *A Theory of Justice*.[17] For Rawls, shame is an emotion felt upon the loss of self-esteem. Self-esteem, in his view, is rooted in the belief that one's aims and ideals are worthy and that one has the personal capacities—the abilities, talents, and qualities of character—one needs to pursue such ideals. Shame is called forth by the recognition either that one lacks these capacities or that one's aims themselves are unworthy. But Deigh disagrees: He invites us to imagine situations in which the loss of self-esteem occasioned by the realization that one has failed to realize an important goal is productive of sorrow, perhaps, but not necessarily of shame; moreover, he notes that we may feel ashamed of something about ourselves (e.g., an outlandish name or our table manners) which may be quite unconnected to what Rawls regards as the ordinary sources of self-esteem. Deigh notes that shame is often occasioned by the recognition that we have violated norms appropriate to our station in society: In such a case, "the subject neither realizes that his aims and ideals are shoddy nor discovers a defect in himself that makes him ill-suited to pursue them."[18] Rawls's mistake was to have associated identity too closely with achievement: He makes no distinction between "who one is and how one conducts one's life."[19] This omission reflects the privilege of "persons who are relatively free of constraints on their choice of life pursuits owing to class, race, ethnic origins," and, I would add, to gender.[20] In my view, Deigh's way of characterizing shame marks an advance over Rawls's, recognizing as it does the extent to which the worth of persons is determined not only by their achievements as measured against their ideals, but by something which may have little to do with their achievements, namely, their "status in the context of some social hierarchy."[21] One disclaimer, however: I find that the subjunctive mood in which Deigh's definition is formulated fails to distinguish sufficiently between shame as a response to demeaning treatment one fears one would invite in appearing to be a person of lesser worth and the shame of someone subjected routinely to such treatment. There are important issues at stake in the quarrel between Deigh and Rawls; I shall return to them later.

Shame, then, involves the distressed apprehension of oneself as a lesser creature. Guilt, by contrast, refers not to the subject's nature but to her actions: Typically, it is called forth by the active violation of principles which a person values and by which she feels herself bound. Deigh puts it well: "Shame is felt over shortcomings, guilt over wrongdoings."[22] Shame is called forth by the apprehension of some serious flaw in the self, guilt by the consciousness that one has committed a transgression. The widely held notion that shame is a response to external and guilt to internal sanctions is incorrect: Shame and guilt are alike in that each involves a condemnation of the self by itself for some failure to measure up; it is the measures that differ. While useful conceptual distinctions can be drawn between shame and guilt, the boundaries between them tend to blur in actual experience. Psychological studies have shown that most people are hard put to state the difference between shame and guilt, nor can they easily classify their experiences under one heading or the other.[23] This is hardly surprising, since each must call forth the other with great frequency. The violation of a cherished moral principle is likely to be taken by anyone without satanic ambitions as the sign of some shameful weakness in the personality.

III

Textbooks on the psychology of women tend to confirm the everyday observation that women are in general less assertive than men, have lower self-esteem, less overall confidence, and poorer self-concepts.[24] The terms on this list refer to traits and dispositions such as assertiveness and to beliefs: To have a poor self-concept, presumably, is to have one set of beliefs about oneself, while to have a good self-concept is to have another. Missing here is any sense of the affective taste, the emotional coloration of these traits and beliefs. Certainly, everyone understands how painful it is to have low self-esteem or too little confidence. Let us pursue this: What, precisely, is the character of this pain?

Several years ago, I taught an upper-level extension course in a suburban high school. The students were mostly high school teachers, required by their school district to earn periodic graduate credit as a condition of continuing employment. None of the students was very young: Most were in their forties and fifties. Women outnumbered men by about two to one. The women, who tended on the average to be somewhat better students than the men, displayed far less confidence in their ability to master the material. I found this surprising, since the female teachers, authorities in their own classrooms, did the same work as the male teachers, had comparable seniority, similar educational credentials, and, I assume, pay equity. The school in which both men and women taught had an excellent reputation. There is nothing unique about the classroom I am about to describe: I have observed in other classrooms what I observed there. I select this particular class as an example because male and female students were mature and well-matched professionally and because their relationships seemed to be free of the sexual tensions and courtship games that sometimes complicate the relationships of younger men and women.

Though women were in the majority, they were noticeably quieter in class discussion than the men. The men engaged freely in classroom exchanges and seemed quite confident—in view of the quality of some of their remarks, over-confident. Women who did enter discussion spoke what linguists call "women's language": Their speech was marked by hesitations and false starts; they tended to introduce their comments with self-denigrating expressions ("You may think that this is a stupid question, but . . ."); they often used a questioning intonation which in effect turned a simple declarative sentence into a request for help or for affirmation from without; they used "tag" questions which had the same effect ("Camus's theme in *The Myth of Sisyphus* is the absurdity of human existence, isn't it?") and excessive qualifiers ("Isn't it true that sometimes, maybe . . .").[25] This style of speaking, whatever its substance, communicates to listeners the speaker's lack of confidence in what she is saying, and this in turn damages her credibility.

In addition to their style of speech, I was struck by the way many female students behaved as they handed me their papers. They would offer heartfelt apologies and copious expressions of regret for the poor quality of their work—work which turned out, most of the time, to be quite good. While apologizing, a student would often press the edges of her manuscript together so as to make it literally smaller, holding the paper uncertainly somewhere in the air as if unsure whether she wanted to relinquish it at all. Typically, she would deliver the apology with head bowed, chest hollowed, and shoulders hunched slightly forward. The male students would stride over to the desk and put down their papers without comment.

Now every female student did not behave in this way all of the time. Nor is this all that the women communicated. To the casual observer, the atmosphere in the classroom was both relaxed and stimulating: Both men and women took an evident interest in the material and managed a lively exchange of ideas. But, like an organ-point that sounded faintly but persistently all term, something else was detectable too: It became clear to me that many women students were ashamed of their written work and ashamed to express their ideas in a straight-forward and open manner. Indeed, it would not be unusual for a student just to say, "I'm really ashamed of this paper," while handing it to me. I have no doubt that these utterances were accurate reports of feeling. At the same time, I suspect that they were rituals of self-shaming undertaken in order to bear more easily a shaming they anticipated from me: An ordeal is often easier to endure if we can choose its time and place. These apologies served also to underscore the students' desire to do well in the course, hence, to get into my good books and, by arousing pity in me for such evident emotional distress, to soften my judgment of their work. Behind a facade of friendliness and informality, two very different dramas of relationship to the teacher were being enacted: The men regarded me as a rival or as an upstart who needed to prove herself; the women, as potentially a very punitive figure who needed to be placated and manipulated.

Given the extent to which psychotherapeutic discourse has permeated ordinary speech, it might seem more natural to say that my female students displayed not shame, but "feelings of inadequacy." In point of fact, it is difficult to distinguish the two. To confess to "feelings of inadequacy" is to do more than merely acknowledge one's limitations: It is to admit to having done some suffering in the contemplation of these limitations. I would not say, for example, that I had "feelings of inadequacy" in regard to auto mechanics. What I feel in regard to my ignorance of auto mechanics is indifference, not anguish. If, however, I say that I feel inadequate in regard to something, I imply that according to my own lights, I ought not to be inadequate in regard to this thing and that my real or putative inadequacy pains me. But what is this pain but a species of psychic distress occasioned by a sense of the self as lacking or diminished—just the definition of shame offered earlier? "When you lack what you do not want, there is no shame."[26]

It seems to me that the demeanor of my female students in that suburban classroom bore the characteristic marks of shame, of a shame felt directly or anticipated: In their silence, the necessity for hiding and concealment; in the tentative character of their speech and in their regular apologetics, the sense of self as defective or diminished. The fear of demeaning treatment could be seen in the cringing before an Other from whom such treatment was anticipated; shame could be read even in the physical constriction of their bodies.

Now if the primordial structure of shame is such that one is ashamed of oneself before the Other, who is the Other before whom my female students were ashamed? Since I have a kindly and permissive style and make a point of never subjecting my students to ridicule, let us assume for the sake of argument that I am not this Other. The identity of this Other, whoever it turns out to be, will be hugely overdetermined, for women in a sexist society are subjected to demeaning treatment by a variety of Others; they bring to the classroom a complex experience of subordination and an elaborate repertoire of stereotyped gestures appropriate to their station. One wonders too whether there is any relationship between women's shame—both the shame that is directly linked to embodiment and the shame that is not—to the persistence of religious traditions that have historically associated female sexuality with pollution and contagion. But whatever the character of this overdetermination, it remains the case that female subjectivity is not constructed entirely elsewhere and then brought ready-made to the classroom: The classroom is also a site of its constitution. What I shall suggest in the next section is that the Other so feared by my female students is, to a surprising degree—especially in light of the overdetermination of shame to which I have just referred—a composite portrait of other and earlier class-room teachers who had, in fact, subjected them but not their male counterparts to consistent shaming behavior. It should be kept in mind in what follows that the classroom is perhaps the *most* egalitarian public space that any woman in our society will ever inhabit.

IV

The Project on the Status and Education of Women of the Association of American Colleges has produced an extraordinary report which details the many ways in which the classroom climate at all educational levels may produce a diminished sense of self in girls and women. While every instructor is by no means guilty of the kinds of demeaning treatment described in the report, such treatment is widespread and pervasive. The report itself is well documented, its claims supported by a variety of empirical studies.[27]

Females, it turns out, are less likely to be called upon directly than males; indeed, women and girls are often ignored, even when they express a willingness to speak. Teachers in grade school talk to boys wherever they are in the room, to girls only when they are nearby. Teachers tend to remember the names of male students better and to call upon them by name more often. Women are not given the same length of time as men to answer questions, suggesting that they are less able to think a problem through and come up with an answer. Nor are men and women asked the same kinds of questions: Women are often asked factual questions (''When did Camus publish *The Stranger*?'') while men are asked questions that require some critical or analytical ability (''What do you see as the major thematic differences between *The Stranger* and *The Plague*?'') Some instructors may make ''helpful'' comments to women that imply, nevertheless, women's lesser competence (''I know that women have trouble with technical concepts but I'll try to help you out''). Instructors tend to coach men more than women, nodding and gesturing more often in response to men's comments and pushing and probing for a fuller response. This suggests that the points men make in discussion are important and that they can stretch themselves intellectually if they try. Women may well receive less praise than men for work of the same quality, for studies have shown repeatedly that work when ascribed to a man is rated higher than the same work when ascribed to a woman, whether the work in question is a scholarly paper, a short story, or a painting. There is evidence that men's success generally is viewed as deserved, women's as due to luck or to the easiness of the task.[28]

Women are interrupted more than men both by their teachers and by their fellow students. Teachers are likelier to use a tone of voice that indicates interest when talking to men but to adopt a patronizing or dismissive tone when talking to women. Teachers have been observed to make more eye contact with men than with women; they may assume a posture of attentiveness when men speak but look away or look at the clock when women speak.

Ignorant of the fact that styles of communication are gender-related, instructors may assume that women's use of ''women's language'' means that women have nothing to say. On the other hand, women may be viewed negatively when they display stereotypically masculine traits such as ambition, assertiveness, or a pleasure in disputation. The female student may receive direct sexual overtures in the classroom, but even if this does not happen, she is far likelier than her male counterpart to receive comments about her appearance. This may suggest to her that she is primarily a decorative being who is less serious and hence less competent than the men in her class.

Instructors may use sexist humor or demeaning sexual allusions to ''spice up'' a dull subject. They may disparage women or groups of women generally.

Or they may use sexist language, referring to human beings in generic masculine terms or calling male students "men" but female students "girls" or "gals." The linguistic disparagement of women may be echoed in a course content from which the history, literature, accomplishments, or perspectives of women have been omitted.

Here, as elsewhere, women of color are in double jeopardy, for the demeaning treatment that is visited upon women, whatever their race, is similar in many ways to the demeaning treatment that is suffered by students of color, whatever their gender. Instructors may interpret students' behavior in the light of racial stereotypes, taking, for example, the silence of a black woman as "sullenness," of a Hispanic woman as "passivity." Black women, in particular, report that their instructors expect them to be either academically incompetent or else academically brilliant "exceptions." A black woman may be singled out, in ways that underscore her sense of not belonging, by being asked for the "black woman's point of view" on some issue rather than her own view.

College teachers have been better mentors to men than to women; they are likelier to choose men for teaching and research assistantships and to contact men when professional opportunities arise. In laboratory courses, instructors have been observed to position themselves closer to men than to women, giving men more detailed instructions on how to do an assignment. They are likelier to do the assignment for women or just allow them to fail. In such courses, men are often allowed to crowd out women at demonstrations. Classroom teachers are unlikely to recognize, hence to try to alter the dynamics of mixed-sex group discussion which are no different in the classroom than they are elsewhere:

> Despite the popular notion that in everyday situations women talk more than men, studies show that in formal groups containing men and women: men talk more than women; men talk for longer periods and take more turns at speaking; men exert more control over the topic of conversation; men interrupt women much more frequently than women interrupt men and men's interruptions of women more often introduce trivial or inappropriately personal comments that bring the woman's discussion to an end or change its focus.[29]

These behaviors, considered *in toto,* cannot fail to diminish women, to communicate to them the insignificance and lack of seriousness of their classroom *personae.* When one considers the length of this catalogue of microbehaviors and senses what must be its cumulative effect, one is tempted to regard the shaming behavior visited upon women in the modern classroom as the moral equivalent of the dunce-cap of old.

The classroom, as we noted earlier, is only one of many locations wherein the female sense of self is constituted. Behaviors akin to the ones just listed are enacted in many other domains of life, in, e.g., family, church, and workplace.

If, as I claimed earlier, women are more shame-prone than men, the cause is not far to seek: Women, more often than men, are made to feel shame in the major sites of social life. Moreover, it is in the act of being shamed and in the feeling ashamed that there is disclosed to women who they are and how they are faring within the domains they inhabit, though, as we shall see, this disclosure is ambiguous and oblique.

V

A number of contemporary philosophers have maintained that ''over a wide range of emotions, beliefs are constitutive of the experience in question.''[30] The so-called emotions of self-assessment, such as pride, shame, and guilt, seem to lend themselves well to analysis in terms of belief. DeSousa, for example, holds that shame appears ''to be founded entirely on belief,'' a view, as we saw earlier, that Rawls seems to share.[31] Now what are the relevant beliefs in which shame is said to consist? Gabrielle Taylor offers an account of the common structure of belief in emotions of self-assessment: ''In experiencing any one of these emotions, the person concerned believes of herself that she has deviated from some norm and that in doing so, she has altered her standing in the world.''[32] Presumably, then, shame would consist in three beliefs: first, the general belief that deviation from *this* norm marks someone as a person of lesser worth; second, the belief that *I* have deviated from this norm; third, the belief that in so doing I have altered my standing in the world.

If this analysis is correct, one would expect students who behave as if they feel *generally* ashamed of their performance to believe in their general failure to measure up to the ordinary standards of academic performance. Now I do not think that my students held any such general beliefs about themselves at all; indeed, I suspect that if confronted with such a claim, they would angrily deny it. Could they not point to evidence of past academic accomplishment? Seemingly ashamed, they do not believe they have anything in general to be ashamed of; it is merely *this* paper, so hastily written she's ashamed to give you, *that* remark she fears you'll find stupid. My students felt inadequate without really believing themselves to be inadequate in the salient respects: They sensed something inferior about themselves without believing themselves to be generally inferior at all.

What transpires in the classroom, it should be noted, goes on behind everyone's back. The shaming behavior is typically quite subtle, so much so that those responsible for it are largely unaware of what they are doing. Students believe that the classroom is a meritocracy, teachers that they treat all students fairly, irrespective of race, class, or gender. Both are wrong. The biases that invade consciousness are so pervasive and so little available to consciousness that they can sabotage good intentions—or even good politics. Hence, the earlier assumption that I myself had done nothing to provoke shame in my female students is very likely wrong as well. Without an alternative interpretive framework wherein their meanings might be differently understood, the comment on a student's appearance is merely a compliment, the sexist joke, mere harmless fun. Because the sexist messages of the classroom are transmitted in a disguised fashion or else both sent and received below the level of explicit awareness, what gets communicated to women does not take the form of propositional meaning and what they take away from the situation is not so much a belief as a *feeling* of inferiority or a *sense* of inadequacy. Female self-awareness in the situation I describe is importantly constituted by a certain contradiction between appearance and reality: on the one hand, the presumption of equality on the part of all actors in this drama, on the other hand, its actual though covert and unacknowledged absence. An ambiguous situation, affirming women in some ways and diminishing them in others, holding itself out as fair while oftentimes violating its own standards of fairness, tends to produce in women a confused and divided consciousness: Believing themselves to be fully the competitive equals of men, many women yet feel somehow diminished and inadequate, this in the absence of any actual evidence of failure.

It is customary in the literature of moral psychology to distinguish between "genuine" or "true" shame and "false" shame. Is what my students were feeling, then, "false" shame? For Arnold Isenberg, we suffer false shame when the lack of what we value has little or no value.[33] Consider, for example, the shame of a Nazi who feels a sudden compassion for his victim. This shame is false in that the standard which the Nazi feels he has betrayed—a standard of utter ruthlessness—has no claim whatever to our moral allegiance. But no such false values are involved in my students' shame; here, the standards in question are no more that the ordinary standards of academic accomplishment, standards that have some claim, at least, to the allegiance of reasonable people. Of course, reasonable people can and do disagree about what ought to be the proper standards of academic performance, but that is not what is at stake here.

Given her commitment to a cognitive theory of shame, for Gabriele Taylor, false shame involves, not surprisingly, a cognitive error. False shame is felt when a person evaluates her behavior in line with commitments which are not really her own, commitments which disturb a moral equilibrium to which she will shortly return. The error here does not, as with Isenberg, consist in the falling away from some absolute standard of value, but in an agent's confusion between commitments which, on balance, reflect her dominant moral sentiments and commitments which do not. "False shame or irrational guilt exert pressures to be a self which is not the agent's genuine self."[34] So, for example, I may find myself covered in shame at the embassy dinner when it is pointed out to me that I am ignorant of the proper employment of the fish fork, but on reflection and on balance, I realize that my genuine commitments incline me to scorn that set of social relations in which the privileged few are taught such things as the proper employment of fish forks. But I do not think my students' case can be assimilated to this kind of case, either. To be falsely shame-prone or shame-ridden, on Taylor's analysis, would be to employ alien standards consistently. But if people were to employ alien standards consistently, how could they be said to *have* genuine standards at all? What becomes of the difference? Moreover, while it is of course the case that the actual standard by which my students fail to measure up—the standard of brute maleness—is a standard alien to any reasonable conception of fairness and therefore alien to my students' genuine moral commitments, Taylor's false shame paradigm sheds no light at all on who applies this standard or how it gets applied. The application of such a standard is certainly a mistake. But it is unilluminating to construe this mistake as a mistake made by these women themselves in the course of mistaking their "false" for their "true" selves.

In sum, then, the "feelings" and "sensings" that go to make up the women's shame I describe, do not reach a state of clarity we can dignify as belief. For all that, they are profoundly disclosive of women's "Being-in-the-world," far more so than many fully formed beliefs women hold about themselves and about their situation, beliefs, for example, that, like men, they enjoy "equality of opportunity" or that the school or workplace is meritocratic in character. What gets grasped in the having of such feelings in nothing less than women's subordinate status in a hierarchy of gender, their situation not in ideology but in the social formation as it is actually constituted. Not only does the revelatory character of shame not occur at the level of belief, but the corrosive character of shame and of similar sensings, their undermining effect and the peculiar helplessness women exhibit when in their power, lies in part in the very failure of these feelings to attain to the status of belief. Once elevated to the relative lucidity of propositional belief, the suspicion that one's papers are poor, one's remarks stupid, indeed, that one's entire academic performance is substandard, would quickly vanish, overwhelmed by a mass of contrary evidence. With the collapse of these suspicions-cum-beliefs, the shame of which they are said to be constitutive, having no longer any foundation, would just disappear as well.

VI

The moral agent who is standardly the focus of moral psychology is everyone and anyone, no one in particular, i.e., an abstract individual. The fact that certain sorts of agents find themselves routinely in specific social locations, e.g., in relationships of subordination to other persons, is not regarded as germane to the analysis of moral emotion *per se;* contingencies like these are thought to be the province of other, more empirical disciplines. This agent feels shame or judges himself guilty when he perceives that his behavior has fallen short of standards that are importantly his own. This agent is lucid; he knows what he has done and why it is wrong. Moreover, insofar as he sits in judgment upon himself, gives the law unto himself, as it were, he is autonomous, Because his

guilt or shame mark his investment in moral norms, these painful emotions are
occasions for moral reaffirmation.[35]

Now what happens when this account of the moral experience of a moral
agent so conceived is tested against actual life, when we consider not the abstract
individuals of philosophical discourse but real people immersed in the complexi-
ties of everyday life, indeed, the real people I have been considering? It becomes
apparent, first of all, that shame, for such people, is not a blip across the face
of an otherwise undisturbed consciousness. For Rawls, as we have seen, and
for Taylor as well, shame is typically construed as a specific episode in the
agent's history, an intrusion in daily life that brings in its wake an altered
understanding of self:

> The experience of an emotion of self-assessment is also a happening which
> changes the state of things. The change is in the view the agent takes of himself.
> Starting from a set of beliefs or assumptions about himself, his conception of
> some event or state of affairs is such that he has to formulate beliefs about
> himself which conflict with the ones held initially; so he has to alter his view
> of himself.[36]

But it is hard to believe that my female students came to have an altered view
of themselves in my classroom. Could the images of themselves these students
displayed during the course have been so different than the images they brought
with them, or indeed, than the ones with which they left? One wonders when
or where many of these women felt truly confident and free, indeed, unashamed.
The shame of some of these women was not a discrete occurrence, but a perpetual attunement, the pervasive affective taste of a life. While accounts like those
of Taylor and Rawls surely cover many occurrences of shame, one wonders
how they can explain its *persistence*.

Nor is shame of the sort I describe an occasion for moral reaffirmation.
Standard accounts of the emotions of self-assessment suggest to me that moral
psychologists are reassured by our capacity to feel such things as shame and
guilt: "Genuine shame and guilt have a useful function to fulfill" in that they
"are always constructive in the sense of being a pressure towards maintaining
or returning to the equilibrium," where "equilibrium" refers to the ensemble
of a person's moral commitments.[37] Unpleasant though they may be, these
emotions are the price we pay for the very capacity to be moral, for only
persons with an emotional investment in the doing of good deeds could feel
distressed by their misdeeds. The internalization of the strictures that require
us to be good would be difficult, indeed, if we paid no emotional price for
being bad. Hence, "genuine" shame and guilt, on the standard story, make us
better persons: They mark a recommitment to principles.

But shame, for the shame-ridden and shame-prone, is not a penance that
restores the miscreant to the proper moral equilibrium—this, for standard moral

psychology, the normal and ordinary use of shame in ethical life. For such persons, there is no such equilibrium to which to return: "Feeling inadequate" may color a person's entire emotional life. Under conditions of oppression, the oppressed must struggle not only against more visible disadvantages but against guilt and shame as well. It was not for nothing that the movement for black empowerment called not only for black civil rights and economic advancement, but for "black pride." Nor should we forget that this was the movement that needed to invent the slogan "Black is beautiful." What figures in much moral psychology as a disruption in an otherwise undisturbed life is, for whole categories of persons, a pervasive affective attunement, a mode of Being-in-the-world wherein their inferiority is disclosed to inferiorized subjects, though, paradoxically, what is *disclosed* fails, in the typical case, to be *understood*.[38] Better people are not made in this way, only people who are weaker, more timid, less confident, less demanding, and hence more easily dominated. The experience of shame may tend to lend legitimacy to the structure of authority that occasions it, for the majesty of judgment is affirmed in its very capacity to injure. The heightened self-consciousness that comes with emotions of self-assessment may become, in the shame of the oppressed, a stagnant self-obsession. Or shame may generate a rage whose expression is unconstructive, even self-destructive. In all these ways, shame is profoundly disempowering. The need for secrecy and concealment that figures so largely in the shame experience is disempowering as well, for it isolates the oppressed from one another and in this way works against the emergence of a sense of solidarity.

We are now in a position to tear the veil of universality from the abstract agent of moral psychology. The individual whose psychic life is not marked by a pervasive sense of diminishment and for whom emotions of shame or guilt, however painful, are indeed occasions for moral reaffirmation, is by no means Everyman, the anyone who is no one in particular. Moral psychology posits as universal an agent who is specific and quite privileged, an agent whose social location is such that he has the capacity not only to be judged but to judge, not only to be defined by others but to define them as well. This agent has escaped the characteristic sorts of psychological oppression on which modern hierarchies of class, race, and gender rely so heavily. The experience of shame *can* be salutary for such a person because he is not systematically impoverished by the moral economy he is compelled to inhabit.

Moral psychology has told us a story, but not the whole story. With few exceptions, shame is treated by those philosophers whose business it is to explain these things to us almost entirely in its relationship to individual failure and wrongdoing, never in its relationship to oppression. This assumes that the role and character of the "moral emotions" can be read out of individual moral experience in a way that divorces this experience from its political roots. Inasmuch as politics and morality are not so neatly divided, this assumption is false. Amelie Rorty has said that we need a much finer taxonomy of the varieties of emotion.[39] We need as well a political phenomenology of the emotions—an examination of the role of emotion, most particularly of the emotions of self-assessment both in the constitution of subjectivity and in the perpetuation of subjection. I hope in this essay to have pointed toward some pathways that such a study might follow.

7

Feeding Egos and Tending Wounds: Deference and Disaffection in Women's Emotional Labor

> (Male) culture was (and is) parasitical, feeding on the emotional strength of women without reciprocity.
>
> —Shulamith Firestone[1]

I

What does a man want? What, in the conflict-ridden arena of current hetero-sexual relations, does a man want from a woman? I went straight to the horse's mouth for an answer, to men, indeed, to men who claim expertise in the inter-pretation and management of relationships. "What a man is attracted to most deeply in a woman," say the male psychologists Connell Cowan and Melvyn Kinder in their best-selling *Smart Women, Foolish Choices,* "is a magical mix-ture of unadulterated power and tenderness—in equal measure."[2] "Strength, forcefulness, and mastery can be gained," they assure us, "without giving up female tenderness and concern with relationships."[3] This is good news indeed. But elsewhere Cowan and Kinder admit that "whatever men say, most of them still like to control the timing and frequency of lovemaking."[4] Men do not want a sexually aggressive woman but "a woman who will be exquisitely responsive and passionate."[5] An alarm buzzer goes off in my head. "Whatever men say . . .": Is this a warning or a confession? How can a woman have "unadul-terated power" and yet be unable to control the timing and frequency of her own lovemaking? Nor are men attracted by the qualities that make for career success in women: "A woman who has worked hard at an education and career is not necessarily valued higher by men."[6] Once more, "unadulterated power" does not in fact attract, for such power would have to include, would it not, the straight-out exercise of power in the public sphere that is oftentimes the reward of career success? I am perplexed: What *does* a man want? Some sort of power in a woman, but none of the ordinary sorts and, less mysteriously, tenderness, not tenderness *simpliciter* but "female tenderness."

Several dozen best-selling books in popular psychology have appeared in recent years that detail what one writer calls the "love crisis"—what is pre-sumed by the authors of these books to be a crisis in the intimate relationships of men and women.[7] These writers, mostly women, tell a depressing tale of female dependency and male misconduct, often gross misconduct. While their characterizations of the "love crisis" differ in some respects, these accounts converge in one respect: All agree that men supply their women with far less of what in popular psychology is called "positive stroking"—the provision of emotional sustenance—than women supply in return, and all agree that this imbalance is a persistent source of female frustration.

Feminist theorists too have noted the gendered imbalance in the provision of emotional support. Ann Ferguson, for example, has maintained that men's appropriation of women's emotional labor is a species of exploitation akin in important respects to the exploitation of workers under capitalism. Ferguson posits a sphere of "sex-affective production," parallel in certain respects to commodity production in the waged sector. Four goods are produced in this system: domestic maintenance, children, nurturance (of both men and children), and sexuality.[8]

According to Ferguson, economic domination of the household by men is analogous to capitalist ownership of the means of production. The relations of sex-affective production in a male-dominated society put women in a position of unequal exchange. Just as control of the means of production by capitalists allows them to appropriate "surplus value" from workers, i.e. the difference between the total value of the workers' output and that fraction of value produced that workers get in return—so men's privileged position in the sphere of sex-affective production allows them to appropriate "surplus nurturance" from women.[9] So, for example, the sexual division of labor whereby women are the primary childrearers requires a " 'woman as nurturer' sex gender ideal." Girls learn "to find satisfaction in the satisfaction of others, and to place their needs second in the case of a conflict."[10] Men, on the other hand, "learn such skills are women's work, learn to demand nurturance from women yet don't know how to nurture themselves."[11] Women, like workers, are caught within a particular division of labor which requires that they produce more of a good—here, nurturance—than they receive in return.

There is a clear allegation of harm to women in Ferguson's account—the harm of exploitation. Joel Feinberg characterizes exploitation generally as an interpersonal relationship that "involves one party (A) profiting from his relation to another party (B) by somehow 'taking advantage' of some characteristic of B's, or some feature of B's circumstances."[12] In most cases of exploitation, B's interests suffer or her rights are violated, but this need not be the case. Feinberg cites a number of examples in which A exploits B but "B is neither harmed nor benefited in the process."[13] Harmless parasitism is a case in point: Consider the sponger who exploits the generosity of a rich and good-natured patron or the gossip columnist who panders to the vulgar curiosity of the public by reporting the daily activities of some celebrity. The patron may be so rich that he neither minds nor misses the handouts; the celebrity may be utterly indifferent to the publicity.[14]

Now the specific kind of exploitation for which Marxists indict capitalism, and Ferguson patriarchy, is exploitation of the first variety, i.e., a taking advantage in which A's profiting from his relation to B involves substantial damage to B's interests. It is important to understand that for the Marxist, capitalist exploitation involves more than the unequal transfer of value from worker to capitalist. Oftentimes we give more to others than they give us in return—perhaps because we *have* more to give—without feeling ourselves aggrieved or naming ourselves exploited. Indeed, to require an exchange of equivalents in all our dealings with other people reduces the richness and variety of human relationship to the aridity of mere contract.

But, so it is charged, the appropriation of surplus value under capitalism involves an unequal exchange that is not at all benign, for the character of this exchange is such as to bring about the systematic disempowerment of one party to the exchange—the direct producers. The appropriation of surplus value is at the root of the workers' alienation, where by "alienation" is meant the loss of control both of the product of labor and of the productive process itself; the loss of autonomy in production brings with it a diminution in the workers' powers, for example, the atrophy of human capacity that attends a lifetime of repetitive or uncreative work. The appropriation of surplus value forms the basis, as well, of the social, political, and cultural preeminence of the appropriating classes.[15]

Ferguson's argument does not require that the two sets of relationships—workers under capitalism, women in the contemporary household—be identical, as clearly they are not. Her claim, as I understand it, is that both are exploited in the same *sense,* i.e., that both are involved in relationships of unequal exchange in which the character of the exchange is itself disempowering. Now this claim is problematical. First, there is some question whether the imbalance in the provision of emotional sustenance is a relationship of unequal exchange at all. Does it, in other words, satisfy the Marxist's first condition for exploitation? Under capitalism, so Marxists claim, workers receive less of the same kind of thing—value—than they give. Moreover, since the value of the worker's wage can be calculated in the same terms as the value of the worker's product, the difference between the two can be quantified and the exploitative character of the relationship just displayed for all to see. Nor, according to Marxists, is there anything else, i.e., anything other than what can be calculated as "value" in Marxist theory that the capitalist gives the worker that might balance the books. Now in order for "surplus nurturance" to be parallel to "surplus value," the intimate exchanges of men and women will have to be shown not only to involve an imbalance in the provision of one *kind* of thing—here nurturance—but not to involve an exchange of equivalents of any sort. But this is just what conservatives deny. The emotional contributions of men and women to intimacy certainly differ, they admit, but their contributions to one another, looked at on a larger canvas, *balance: He* shows his love for her by bringing home the bacon, *she* by securing for him a certain quality of nurturance and concern. Might they be right?[16]

Second, even if women's provision of emotional care to men can be shown not to be embedded within a larger exchange of equivalents, is it clear that women are really harmed by providing such care? Are the men who take more than they give in return anything worse than Feinberg's mere harmless parasites whose exploitation fails to issue in any genuine damage? Differently put, does the situation of women in intimacy satisfy the Marxist's second condition for exploitation, i.e., that there be not only an unequal transfer of powers but a genuine disempowerment in consequence of this transfer? Many feminists have condemned the classic bargain between man and woman (economic support in return for domestic labor and emotional caregiving) on the grounds that economic dependency itself is disempowering. But is it possible to argue that the unreciprocated provision of emotional sustenance—"female tenderness"—is disempowering *in and of itself?* And if it is, in what, precisely, does this disempowerment consist?

II

Let us fix with more precision the character of the emotional sustenance that women are said to provide more of to men than they receive in return. What is it, in the ideal case, to give someone "emotional support?" To support someone emotionally is to keep up his spirits, to keep him from sinking under the weight of burdens that are his to bear. To sink would be to fail to cope at all, to fall prey to paralysis or despair, in less extreme cases, to cope poorly. To give such support, then, is to tend to a person's state of mind in such a way as to make his sinking less likely; it is to offer him comfort, typically by the bandaging up of his emotional wounds or to offer him sustenance, typically by the feeding of his self-esteem. The aim of this supporting and sustaining is to produce or to maintain in the one supported and sustained a conviction of the value and importance of his own chosen projects, hence of the value and importance of his own person.

It is the particular quality of a caregiver's attention that can bolster the Other's confidence. This attention can take the form of speech, of praise, perhaps for the Other's character and accomplishments, or it can manifest itself in the articulation of a variety of verbal signals (sometimes called "conversational cheerleading") that incite him to continue speaking, hence reassuring him of the importance of what he is saying. Or such attention can be expressed nonverbally, e.g., in the forward tilt of the caregiver's body, the maintaining of eye contact, the cocking of her head to the side, the fixing of a smile upon her face.

Again, the work of emotional healing can be done verbally in a myriad of ways, from simple expressions of indignation at what the boss has said about him, to the construction of elaborate rationales that aim, by reconceptualizing them, to make his failures and disappointments less terrible; or nonverbally, in the compassionate squeezing of a hand or in a hug, in the sympathetic furrowing of a brow, or in a distressful sighing. The work of emotional repair—the tending of wounds—and the bolstering of confidence—the feeding of egos—overlap in many ways. A sustained sympathetic listening, as we have seen, conveys to the speaker the importance of what he is saying, hence the suggestion that he himself is important; beyond this, a willingness to listen in comforting, for hurts, if hurts there are, sting less when we can share them. To enter feelingly and without condescension into another's distress—a balm to the spirit indeed—is to affirm that person's worth, though an affirmation of someone's worth need not require any particular effort at emotional restoration. Affection is also a factor in the provision of emotional support. While emotional support might be forthcoming from some stranger on a train in whom I decide to confide, the forms of emotional caregiving as they have been described here are among the commonest ways we show affection, especially when the caregiving is under-scored, as it is among intimates, by loving endearments.

In our society, women in most social locations stand under an imperative to provide emotional service to men, and many chafe at the failure of men to provide such service in return. Lillian Rubin's sensitive study of working-class marriage, *Worlds of Pain* (1976), reveals that issues of relationship and inti-macy, once thought to be the province of the middle class, have now spread to other socioeconomic groups as well.[17] The wives in Rubin's study complain of the emotional unavailability of their men in tones not very different than those sounded by the professional therapists who write popular psychology relation-ship manuals for a middle-class audience. Such complaints are strikingly absent from what was for years the landmark study of working-class couples, Mirra Komarovsky's *Blue-Collar Marriage* (1962).[18] With increasing geographic mo-bility, the erosion of older working-class communities and of the networks of kin they once housed, working-class couples are thrown increasingly onto their own emotional resources; these circumstances, as well as the powerful cultural influence of middle-class values and styles of life, combine to bring forth new demands and, with them, new discontents.

Black women have come under particular attack for an alleged deficiency of "female tenderness." Some black men have laid part of their troubles at the door of the black woman: She is too critical, too aggressive, too hard, a castrator who not only fails to "stand behind her man" but actively undermines him.[19] These charges, fueled by the relative economic independence of the black woman, became particularly virulent during the emergence, in the late sixties, of the Black Power movement and of various black nationalist and separatist movements; this led to an extended and acrimonious discussion among politically conscious black women and men.[20] Though far poorer overall than white women, black women as a group tend to be less economically dependent on black men than white women are on white men and more likely to be heads of their own households. This absence of dependency often bespeaks hardship, tied as it is to black men's poverty and to the material deprivation of whole communities, but it translates too into female self-assertion and a refusal to submit to domestic tyranny. The common and continuing complaints about black female assertion suggest that once again, the style and values of the white middle class are trend setting for American society as a whole. The fact that her behavior was condemned for its alleged failure to conform to the norms of the oppressor was an irony not lost on the black woman.[21]

Emotional caregiving can be done as an expression of love or friendship. It can also be done for pay as part of one's job. Either way, it involves the same two elements—the feeding of egos and the nursing of wounds. But commercial caregiving can differ significantly from the deeper connections between intimates. In a detailed study of the emotional work done by flight attendants, Arlie Hochschild has given a fine account of the "commercialization of human feeling."[22] These mostly female workers are paid to generate commercial affection for passengers: to smile steadily and to lay down around themselves an atmosphere of warmth, cheerfulness, and friendly attention. A relentless cheerfulness would be difficult enough to sustain under any circumstances, but it has become even harder with the speed-up associated with airline deregulation. Not only must the attendant's emotional care be expended on many more passengers per flight, but the passengers themselves are often stressed, feeling the effects of longer lines, lost baggage, and late flights.[23]

Attendants must manage not only their passengers' feelings, but their own as well: They must work to "induce or suppress feeling in order to sustain the outward countenance that produces the proper state of mind in others."[24] Work it is too, for "to show that the enjoyment takes effort is to do the job poorly."[25] A commercial logic penetrates "deeper and deeper into what we used to think of as a private, psychological, sacred part of a person's self and soul."[26] What often results is a flight attendant's feeling of falseness or emptiness, an estrangement from her own feeling self, even a confusion as to what or whether she is feeling anything at all. The flight attendant's sense of inauthenticity, worsened by the physical and psychological effects of speed-up generally, can contribute to depression, insomnia, alcoholism, and drug abuse.[27] Under such conditions, the provision of emotional service can be disempowering indeed.

But the emotional sustenance women give men in relationships of intimacy resembles commercial caregiving only very superficially. True, the flight attendant, like the good wife, must feed egos and heal wounds; she is supposed to make every passenger feel wanted and important and to deal with whatever distress is occasioned by the stresses of travel. But the one relationship is casual and brief, the other more enduring and profound. Intimate relationships require more complex sensitivities and engage more aspects of the self. The woman in intimacy feels deep affection for the one she supports; she is sincere and heartfelt in providing what she provides; she loses herself, so to speak, in her work. Of course, caregiving in intimate relationships can sometimes come to *feel* just as mechanical as it does for the flight attendant in speed-up, a performance from which the woman herself feels increasingly remote. But intimate relationships in which this happens are surely in trouble; indeed, any relationship in which this occurs consistently hardly qualifies as an intimate relationship at all. Now one can well understand how the routine emotion work of flight attendants may become disempowering, leading as it often does to self-estrangement, an inability to identify one's own emotional states, even to drug abuse or alcoholism. But how can the provision of affectionate regard and the sympathetic tending of psychic wounds—activities that require the exercise of such virtues as loving-kindness and compassion—be disempowering too? Surely, the opportunity to attend to the Other in these ways must be morally empowering for it gives us the chance not merely to be good by doing good, but to become morally better through the cultivation and exercise of important moral qualities. And are we not privileged, too, in being allowed entrée into the deepest psychological recesses of another, in being released, if only temporarily, from the burden of isolation and loneliness that each of us must bear? The claim that women in intimacy are disempowered in their provision of emotional support to men may begin to seem not merely mistaken, but perverse. But let us look more closely.

III

A number of feminist theorists have treated women's unequal provision of emotional caregiving to men as a zero-sum game: Men, they assume are empowered and women disempowered in proportion to the immediate emotional benefits—the feeding of egos, the tending of wounds—that men gain from an emotional service they do not fully reciprocate. Metaphors of filling and emptying are often used to describe this state of affairs: Women fill men with our energies; this filling strengthens men and depletes ourselves.[28] Moreover, the psychic benefits men gain from women's caregiving make them fitter to rule; in dispensing these benefits, women only make themselves fitter to obey.

There is no quarreling with the claim that men as a group receive direct psychological benefits from women's emotional sustenance: This seems obvious. But in my view, this standard view errs on two counts. First, I suspect that many feminist thinkers overestimate the efficacy of female nurturance. I shall pursue the question of the extent and effect of female emotional support in the balance of this section. Second, I believe that the standard view underestimates the subjectively disempowering effects of unreciprocated caregiving on women themselves, quite apart from the question how and to what extent men may be psychologically empowered by receiving it. It may be the case that women's nurturance is not a zero-sum game, i.e., that, in many circumstances, women may disempower themselves more in the giving of emotional support than men are empowered in the getting of it. I shall examine the question of women's subjective disempowerment in Sections IV and V below.

One variant of what I have been calling the "standard view" is "the safety-valve theory." The claim is sometimes made that women's emotional caregiving does more than secure psychological benefits to individual men: This caregiving is said to shore up the patriarchal system as a whole by helping to stabilize the characteristic institutions of contemporary patriarchal society. These institutions, it is claimed, are marked by hierarchy, hence by unequal access to power, and by impersonality, alienated labor, and abstract instrumental rationality. Now men pay a heavy price for their participation in such a system, even though the system as such allows men generally to exercise more power than women generally. The disclosure of a person's deepest feelings is dangerous under conditions of competition and impersonality: A man runs the risk of displaying fear or vulnerability if he says too much. Hence, men must sacrifice the possibility of frank and intimate ties with one another; they must abandon the possibility of emotional release in one another's company. Instead, they must appear tough, controlled, and self-sufficient, in command at all times.

Now, so the argument goes, the emotional price men pay for participation in this system would be unacceptably high, were women not there to lower it. Women are largely excluded from the arenas wherein men struggle for prestige; because of this and by virtue of our socialization into patterns of nurturance, women are well situated to repair the emotional damage men inflict on one another. Women's caregiving is said to function as a "safety valve" that allows the release of emotional tensions generated by a fundamentally inhuman system. Without such release, these tensions might explode the set of economic and political relationships wherein they are now uneasily contained. Hence, women are importantly involved in preventing the destabilization of a system in which some men oppress other men and men generally oppress women generally.[29] Does this theory, the "safety-valve" theory of female nurturance, pinpoint what is chiefly disempowering about the unbalanced provision of emotional sustenance? How persuasive is it anyhow?

Hegel says that no man may be a hero to his valet. Surely, though, many men are heroes to their wives. But consider the following: While it is good to have one's importance affirmed, even by an underling, how valuable is it, in the last analysis, when such affirmation issues from one's social inferior? "Praise from Caesar is praise indeed"—but she isn't Caesar. Women, after all, are out of the action: Typically, we lack standing in the world. We have too little prestige ourselves to be a source of much prestige for men. Most men look to other men for the determination of their status and for an affirmation of personal worth that really counts. When such affirmation is not forthcoming, the tender concern of women must offer some consolation, but how much?

Moreover, we must remember that men are able to do without the emotional support of women for long periods of time, in prison, for example, or in the army. In an absorbing study of the current social and psychological dimensions of friendship, Lillian Rubin claims that even though men's relationships with other men do not typically exhibit the marks of intimacy—for her, verbal disclosure of feeling and significant emotional display—men are able nonetheless to bond with other men and that this bonding, in its own way, can become a significant source of emotional support. Men, she says,

> can live quite robustly without intimacy—an emotional connection that ties two people together in important and powerful ways. At the most general level, the shared experience of maleness—of knowing its differences from femaleness, of affirming those differences through an intuitive understanding of each other that needs no words—undoubtedly creates a bond between men. It's often a primitive bond, a sense of brotherhood that may be dimly understood, one that lives side by side with the more easily observable competitive strain that exists in their relations as well.[30]

Competition among men may not only *not* be a source of male emotional distress that requires female caregiving to "bind" its potentially destabilizing effects, but may itself be a powerful impetus to male bonding and a profound source of male self-esteem. One of her respondents has this to say about competition: "It's not that I don't feel comfortable with women, but I enjoy men in a special way. I enjoy competing with men. I don't like to compete with women: there's no fun in it."[31] When Rubin asks him what precisely he enjoys about competition, here is his reply:

> (Laughing) Only a woman would ask that. (Then more seriously) It's hard to put into words. I can strut my stuff, let myself go all the way. I really get off on that; its exciting. It doesn't make much difference whether it's some sport or getting an account, I'm playing to win. I can show off just how good I am.[32]

I am concerned in this paper with men who are capable of accepting emotional sustenance from women but who do not return what they are given. Now the best-sellers I referred to earlier complain, to be sure, of inequalities in the provision of emotional suport, but they are much more exercized about men's emotional anemia—men's inexpressiveness and fear of self-disclosure, in a word, their *refusal* even to accept sustenance from their women. And this makes sense: Tough guys, confined since childhood to a narrow range of acceptable masculine emotion, cannot easily become emotionally expressive—even with a woman. But perhaps this way of formulating the situation is misleading, suggesting as it does a dualism of appearance and reality—the appearance of invulnerability without, the reality of a rich, suffering, and needy emotional life within. It is likelier that a taboo on the display of some emotion acts in effect as a refusal of permission to oneself even to feel it. Thus, there appear to be psychological mechanisms in men that tend, quite independently of female emotional nurturance, to "cool out" such potentially destabilizing emotions as resentment, grief, or frustration. Even if we assume that such emotions have not been anaesthetized, but are only simmering below the surface of a man incapable of sharing them with a woman, there is no evidence that emotionally inexpressive men are more rebellious than their less repressed counterparts. All kinds of men are rebels, the expressive and the inexpressive alike, men who take emotional sustenance from women without recompense, even the minority of men who know how to return what they are given. Nor is there evidence that in periods of political ferment, widespread resistance on the part of men to given conditions is correlated in any way with a breakdown or diminution in the provision of female nurturance—a correlation that the "safety-valve" theory would seem to suggest.

The better mental and physical health of married men is often cited as evidence that men receive very significant benefits from women's emotional caregiving. It has been assumed that the emotional support men receive from their wives may explain why married men live longer than single men and why they score lower on standard indices of psychopathology.[33] But even here, some scepticism may be in order. The greater longevity of married men, for example, may be due as much to better physical care (regular meals, better nutrition, more urging from the wife to seek medical help) as to wives' provision of emotional care. Moreover, it isn't clear whether the superior mental health of married men is due to female emotional caretaking or whether marriage as an institution selects men who are sufficiently stable to receive these benefits in the first place. And even in relationships of some duration, there are tragic cases in which every resource of a woman's loving attention is ineffective against what are arguably the effects of the stressful circumstances of her man's life—alcoholism, drug addiction, depression, or suicide. Contemplation of the scale on which these tragedies are repeated may generate, again, some scepticism as to the efficacy of female emotional sustenance.

All these considerations, I think, tell somewhat against the "safety-valve" theory of female caregiving. While there is no doubt that men receive benefits from women's provision of emotional sustenance, and while it is conceivable that this sustenance may to some extent keep the lid on male discontent, these effects may be neither as extensive nor as significant as the safety-valve theory suggests. I think it unlikely that women's disempowerment stands in any very direct proportion either to the concrete emotional benefits that men receive from our emotional labor, or to whatever stabilization men's psychological repair may lend to an oppressive political and economic system. I suggest instead that we look for a disempowerment that is more subtle and oblique, one that is rooted in the subjective and deeply interiorized effects *upon women ourselves* both of the emotional care we give and of the care we fail to get in return.

IV

Love, affection, and the affectionate dispensing of emotional sustenance may seem to be purely private transactions that have nothing to do with the macrosocial domain of status. But this is false. Sociologist Theodore Kemper maintains that "a love relationship is one in which at least one actor gives (or is prepared to give) extremely high status to another actor."[34] "Status accord" he defines as "the voluntary compliance with the needs, wishes or interests of the other."[35] Now insofar as women's provision of emotional sustenance is a species of compliance with the needs, wishes and interests of men, such provision can be understood as a conferral of status, a paying of homage by the female to the male. Consider once again the bodily displays that are typical of women's intimate caregiving: the sympathetic cocking of the head; the forward inclination of the body; the frequent smiling; the urging, through appropriate vocalizations, that the man continue his recital, hence, that he may continue to commandeer the woman's time and attention. I find it suggestive that these behaviors are identical to common forms of deference display in hierarchies of status.[36] But status is not accorded mutually: Insofar as the emotional exchanges in question are contained within a gendered division of emotional labor that does not require of men what it requires of women, our caregiving, in effect, is a collective genuflection by women to men, an affirmation of male importance that is unreciprocated. The consistent giving of what we don't get in return is a performative acknowledgement of male supremacy and thus a contribution to our own social demotion. The implications of this collective bending of the knee, however, rarely enter consciousness. The very sincerity and quality of heartfelt concern that the woman brings to her man's emotional needs serves to reinforce in her own mind the importance of his little dramas of daily life. But he receives her attention as a kind of entitlement; by failing to attend to her in the same way she attends to him, he confirms for her and, just as importantly, for himself, her inferior position in the hierarchy of gender.

Women do not expect mutual recognition from the children we nurture, especially when these children are very young, but given the companionate ideal that now holds sway, we yearn for such recognition from the men with whom we are intimate. Its withholding is painful, especially so since in the larger society it is men and not women who have the power to give or to withhold social recognition generally. Wishing that he would notice; waiting for him to ask: how familiar this is to women, how like waiting for a sovereign to notice a subject, or a rich man, a beggar. Indeed, we sometimes find ourselves begging for his attention—and few things are as disempowering as having to beg.

Women have responded in a number of ways to men's refusal of recognition. A woman may merge with her man psychologically to such an extent that she just claims as her own the joys and sorrows he narrates on occasions of caretaking. She now no longer needs to resent his indifference to her doings, for his doings have just *become* her doings. After eight years of seeing it, we recall the picture easily: Ronald Reagan at the podium, Nancy, a bit behind her husband, fixing upon him a trancelike gaze of total admiration and utter absorption. Here is the perfect visual icon of the attempt to merge one's consciousness with the consciousness of the Other.

Psychologists such as Nancy Chodorow and Dorothy Dinnerstein have maintained that the relational style of women in matters of feeling and our more "permeable ego boundaries" are due to the fact that girls, unlike boys, are not required to sever in the same way their original identification with the maternal caretaker.[37] If this is true, the phenomenon that I am describing may be "overdetermined" by psychological factors. Nevertheless, it is worth asking to what extent the merging of the consciousness of the woman with the object of her emotional care may be a strategy adopted in adult life to avoid anger and the disruption of relationship, effects that might otherwise follow upon the refusal of recognition. Moreover, the successful provision of intimate caregiving itself requires a certain loss of oneself in the Other, whatever the infantile determinants of such merger and whatever the utility such merging may have in the management of anger or resentment. I shall return to this point later.

Women sometimes demand the performance of ritualized gestures of concern from men—the remembering of a birthday or anniversary, a Valentine's Day card—as signs of a male caring that appears to be absent from the transactions of everyday life. The ferocity with which women insist on these ritual observances is a measure, I believe, of our sense of deprivation. If the man forgets, and his forgetting issues in the absence of some object—a present, a Valentine— that cultural rituals have defined as visible and material symbols of esteem, a lack felt privately may be turned into a public affront. Women's preoccupation with such things, in the absence of an understanding of what this preoccupation means, has gained us a reputation for capriciousness and superficiality, a reputation that in itself is disempowering. "Why can't a woman be more like a man?" sings the exasperated Prof. Henry Higgins. "If I forgot your silly birthday, would you fuss? / . . . Why can't a woman be like us?"

Neither of these strategies—minimalism or merger—really works. The woman who accepts a ritualized gesture, performed at most a few times a year and often very perfunctorily, in exchange for the devoted caregiving she provides her man all the time, has made a bad bargain indeed, while the psychological overidentification I describe here is grounded in a self-deceived attempt to deny pain and to avoid the consequences of anger. To attempt such merger is to practice magic or to have a try at self hypnosis. A woman who is economically dependent on a man may find it natural to identify with his interests; in addition to the kind of merging I have described, such dependency itself feeds a tendency to overidentification. But given the generally fragile character of relationships today, the frequency of divorce, and the conflicts that arise even within ongoing relationships, prudence requires that a woman regard the coincidence of her interests with those of her partner as if they were merely temporary.

V

In this section, I shall argue that women run a risk that our unreciprocated caregiving may become both epistemically and ethically disempowering. In the course of her caretaking, a woman may be tempted to adopt morally questionable attitudes and standards of behavior or she may fall prey to a number of false beliefs that tend to mystify her circumstances.

First of all, there is the epistemic risk, i.e., the risk that the woman will accept uncritically "the world according to him" and that she will have corresponding difficulty in the construction of the world according to herself. How does this happen? To support and succor a person is, typically, to enter feelingly into that person's world; it is to see things from his point of view, to enter imaginatively into what he takes to be real and true.[38] Nel Noddings expresses it well: To adopt a caring attitude toward another is to become "engrossed" in that other: it is "a displacement of interest from my own reality to the reality of the other," whereby "I set aside my temptation to analyze and to plan. I do not project; I receive the other into myself, and I see and feel with the other."[39] Hence, caring "involves stepping out of one's own personal frame of reference into the other's."[40] Here is merger of another sort, one not motivated by a failure of recognition but by the very character of emotional caregiving itself.

Now a woman need not merge epistemically with the man she is sustaining on every occasion of caregiving; there are times when she will reject his version of things, either to his face or to herself. But if a caregiver begins *consistently* to question the values and beliefs of the one to whom she is supposed to be offering sustenance, her caregiving will suffer. She is caught in the following paradox: If she keeps her doubts to herself, she runs the risk of developing that sense of distance and falseness that, as we saw earlier, is a major mark of alienated caregiving in commercial settings. If she articulates her doubts, again consistently, likely as not she will be seen as rejecting or even disloyal. Either way, her relationship will suffer. Professional therapists are required to develop a "hermeneutic of suspicion"; our intimates are not. We have the eminently reasonable expectation that our friends and intimates will support our struggles and share our allegiances, rejoice in our victories and mourn our defeats, in a word, that they will see things—at least the big things in our lives—as we see them. And so, an "epistemic lean" in the direction of the object of her solicitude is part of the caregiver's job—of any caregiver's job—it comes, so to speak, with the territory.

"The world according to him": This is that ensemble of meanings that reflect a man's more privileged location in the social totality. Now the antagonism between men and women is only part of the complex system of antagonisms that structure the social order. Hence, there will be many occasions on which his version of things will be the same as her own best version, his picture of things as much a reflection of her interests as his own. For example, black women and men who struggle in common against racism must share, in large measure, an understanding of the society in which their struggle takes place. But unless we posit a *general* identity of interest between men and women, there will be occasions, indeed countless occasions, on which a man's version of what is real and true will reflect his more privileged social location, not hers.

We know from a variety of sources that women in our society lack epistemic authority.[41] The lack has many causes, not the least of which is the historic male monopoly of the means of social interpretation and communication, a monopoly that has only recently been challenged. We typically construe women's assimilation of masculinist ideology in too mechanical and intellectualist a fashion: Mystified and distorted ideas, we think, are transmitted from one location—say, the church or school—and received in another, the woman's mind. What is absent from this picture is women's own active role in the assimilation of men's ideas, our empathic, imaginative, and affective interiorization of a masculine perspective. Since we are dealing, once again, with a clear sexual division of labor, there is no corresponding affirmation, in intimacy, of the world according to *her*.

There is then, a risk for women's epistemic development in our unreciprocated caregiving. What are its risks for our ethical life? Hegel claimed that women's ethical perfectability lay in the family, a position that has been echoed by recent conservative Christian writers.[42] With more perspicacity, John Stuart Mill pointed to the patriarchal family as a source of moral corruption for both men and women: He saw lying, hypocrisy, and self-abasement as the principal dangers for women.[43] Mill's discussion of these dangers is unsurpassed. But I point to another danger still, one that involves neither lying nor self-abasement, one that arises from the sort of heartfelt and committed caregiving that is situated at the farthest reach from hypocrisy.

To affirm a man's sense of reality is at the same time to affirm his values. "Stand by your man": What else can this mean? Recall that male psychologists Cowan and Kinder (*Smart Women, Foolish Choices*) did not ask for high ethical principles in a woman, much less for ethical strenuousness, but for "female tenderness." Tenderness requires compassion and forgiveness, clearly virtues under some circumstances and certainly excellences in a caregiver. But there are situations in which virtues such as forgiveness lead to moral blindness or outright complicity:

> Behind every great man is a woman, we say, but behind every monster there is a woman too, behind each of those countless men who stood astride their narrow worlds and crushed other human beings, causing them hideous suffering and pain. There she is in the shadows, a vague female silhouette, tenderly wiping blood from their hands.[44]

This is vividly expressed, understandingly so, since it appears in a discussion of Teresa Stangl, wife of Fritz Stangl, Kommandant of Treblinka. Teresa, anti-Nazi and a devout Catholic, was appalled by what she knew of her husband's work; nevertheless, she maintained home and hearth as a safe harbor to which he returned when he could; she "stood behind her man." Few of us would take female tenderness to these lengths, but many of us, I suspect, have been morally silenced or morally compromised in small ways because we thought it more important to provide emotional support than to keep faith with our own principles. In such a situation, there is still a felt tension between our own commitments and what we find it prudent to express. More corrosive is a danger that inheres in the very nature of intimate caregiving—the danger of an "ethical lean" that, like the epistemic lean I mentioned earlier, may rob the caregiver herself of a place to stand.

The emotional caregiving provided by the "good wife" or her equivalent is similar in some ways to that furnished by the "good mother." But it is importantly different as well. Insofar as a mother is interested in the preservation, growth, and social acceptability of her child, she must be attentive to the child's moral development; she must, on occasion, show herself capable of "shaping a child according to moral restraints."[45] But a woman's adult partner is not a child, no matter how childishly he may behave; she will be judged by society more for her loyalty than for his morality. A husband—or lover—does not want and will not easily tolerate ethical training from his wife; what he wants instead is her approval and acceptance. William James expressed it most candidly: What the "average American" wants is a wife who will provide him with a

> tranquil spot where he shall be valid absolutely and once for all; where, having been accepted, he is secure from further criticism, and where his good aspirations may be respected no less than if they were accomplished realities.[46]

Women as well as men seek succor and repair in the sphere of intimacy, a "haven in a heartless world" where the damage that has been sustained elsewhere can be repaired. But here, as elsewhere, men's needs are not only likelier to be satisfied than women's needs but satisfied at women's expense. The epistemic and ethical dangers that, if I am correct, inhere in the heartfelt and successful provision of emotional sustenance in intimacy are borne disproportionately by women. Men get the benefits; women run the risks.

VI

Disempowerment, then, may be inscribed in the more prominent features of women's unreciprocated caregiving: in the accord of status and the paying of homage; in the scarcely perceptible ethical and epistemic "leaning" into the reality of one who stands higher in the hierarchy of gender. But this is only part of the story. In this section I want to identify some countertendencies, ways in which women's provision of emotional sustenance to men may *feel* empowering and hence contradict, on a purely phenomenal level, what may be its objectively disempowering character.

Tending to wounds: this is a large part of what it is to provide someone with emotional support. But this means that in one standard scenario of heterosexual intimacy, the man appears to his female caregiver as vulnerable and injured. Fear and insecurity: for many men, these are the offstage companions of competitive displays of masculinity, and they are aspects of men's lives that women know well. To the woman who tends him, this fellow is not only no colossus who bestrides the world, but he may bear little resemblance to the patriarchal oppressor of feminist theory. The man may indeed belong to a more powerful caste; no matter, this isn't what he *seems* to her at the moment. One imagines Frau Stangl's tender clucks of sympathy as the harried Fritz rehearses, greatly edited, the trials and tribulations of his day at work: How put upon he is from above and below, how he suffers!

Why isn't every woman a feminist? (See Chapter 5 above.) Feminism tells a tale of female injury, but the average woman in heterosexual intimacy knows that men are injured too, as indeed they are. She may be willing to grant, this average woman, that men in general have more power than women in general. This undoubted fact is merely a fact; it is *abstract,* while the man of flesh and blood who stands before her is *concrete:* His hurts are real, his fears palpable. And like those heroic doctors on the late show who work tirelessly through the epidemic even though they may be fainting from fatigue, the woman in intimacy may set her own needs to one side in order better to attend to his. She does this not because she is "chauvinized" or has "false consciousness," but because *this is what the work requires.* Indeed, she may even excuse the man's abuse of her, having glimpsed the great reservoir of pain and rage from which it issues. Here is a further gloss on the ethical disempowerment attendant upon women's caregiving: In such a such a situation, a woman may be tempted to collude in her own ill-treatment.[47]

Foucault has claimed that the practice of confession is disempowering to the one who confesses. Confession, as it is practiced in psychoanalysis or religion, is designed to lead the one confessing into the heart of a presumed "true" or "real" self, which he is ever after obligated to claim as his own. But there is no such self: The idea of such a self, says Foucault, is an illusion, a mere device whereby norms are inscribed in the one confessing that secure his subordination to the locus of power represented by the confessor.[48] But here is a counterexample to Foucault's claim: In the case of heterosexual intimacy, confession is disempowering not to the man who confesses but to the woman who hears this confession. How so? The woman is not the agent of any institutional power. She has no authority either to exact penance or to interpret the situation according to norms that could, in effect, increase the prestige of the institution she represents, hence her own prestige. Indeed, the exigencies of female tenderness are such as virtually to guarantee the man's absolution by the woman—not on her terms, but on his. Moreover, the man's confession of fear or failure tends to mystify the woman's understanding not only of the power dimensions of the relationship between herself and this particular man, but of the relations of power between men and women in general.

An apparent reversal has taken place: The man, her superior in the hierarchy of gender, now appears before the woman as the weaker before the stronger, the patient before his nurse. A source within the woman has been tapped and she feels flowing outward from herself a great power of healing and making whole. She imagines herself to be a great reservoir of restorative power. This feeling of power gives her a sense of agency and of personal efficacy that she may get nowhere else. We read that one of Kafka's mistresses, Milena Jesenka, "believed she could cure Kafka of all his ills and give him a sense of well-being simply by her presence—if only he wanted it."[49]

While women suffer from our relative lack of power in the world and often resent it, certain dimensions of this powerlessness may seem abstract and remote. We know, for example, that we rarely get to make the laws or direct the major financial institutions. But Wall Street and the U.S. Congress seem very far away. The power a woman feels in herself to heal and sustain, on the other hand—"the power of love"—is, once again, concrete and very near: It is like a field of force emanating from within herself, a great river flowing outward from her very person.

Thus, a complex and contradictory female subjectivity is constructed within the relations of caregiving. Here, as elsewhere, women are affirmed in some ways and diminished in others (see Chapter 6, p. 94), this within the unity of a single act. The woman who provides a man with largely unreciprocated emotional sustenance accords him status and pays him homage; she agrees to the unspoken proposition that his doings are important enough to deserve substantially more attention than her own. But even as the man's supremacy in the relationship is tacitly assumed by both parties to the transaction, the man reveals himself to his caregiver as vulnerable and insecure. And while she may well be ethically and epistemically disempowered by the care she gives, this caregiving affords her the feeling that a mighty power resides within her being.

The situation of those men in the hierarchy of gender who avail themselves of female tenderness is not thereby altered: Their superordinate position is neither abandoned, nor their male privilege relinquished. The vulnerability these men exhibit is not a prelude in any way to their loss of male privilege or to an elevation in the status of women. Similarly, the feeling that one's love is a mighty force for good in the life of the beloved doesn't make it so, as Milena Jesenka found, to her sorrow. The *feeling* of out-flowing personal power so characteristic of the caregiving woman is quite different from the *having* of any actual power in the world. There is no doubt that this sense of personal efficacy provides some compensation for the extra-domestic power women are typically denied: If one cannot be a king oneself, being a confidante of kings may be the next best thing. But just as we make a bad bargain in accepting an occasional Valentine in lieu of the sustained attention we deserve, we are ill advised to settle for a mere feeling of power, however heady and intoxicating it may be, in place of the effective power we have every right to exercise in the world.

Finally, a footnote to this discussion of the subjective gratifications of caregiving: In the tending of wounds, is there sometimes an unacknowledged *Schadenfreude*—a pleasure in the contemplation of another's distress—in the sight of the master laid so low? It may or may not be *this* man to whom she is forced to submit, but his vulnerability and dependency may in some sense represent for her the demotion of all men and she may find this symbolic demotion gratifying. Since there is no requirement that our emotional lives exhibit consistency, a mild, quite compensatory *Schadenfreude* may coexist with the most beneficent of motives. But the pleasures of revenge, like the pleasures of merger and self-loss, need to be foregone.

In the provision of emotional sustenance, then, as in the processes of narcissistic self-intoxication, conventional femininity reveals itself as profoundly seductive. (See Chapter 3 above.) Here, as in other aspects of our lives, we are offered real and gratifying feminine satisfactions in return for what this same femininity requires that we renounce. Until alternative sources of gratification can be found, such pleasures may be indeed difficult to renounce.

VII

Some concluding observations are now in order. We may think of relationships of emotional support as lying along a continuum. At one end are the perfunctory and routinized relationships of commercial caregiving in which the caregiver feels no genuine concern for the object of her attention and where, in the worst case, the doing of her job requires that she manipulate, suppress and falsify her own feeling life. At the other end of the continuum lies the caregiving of absolute sincerity; here there is neither an awareness of ulterior motive on the part of the caregiver nor any inner reservation that might compromise the total partisanship and wholehearted acceptance she directs toward the object of her solicitude. Most provisions of emotional support fall somewhere in between. I have chosen to focus on caregiving of the latter kind because I think that its risks have not been fully appreciated and because in most kinds of noncommercial caregiving we take *this* kind as a norm; we measure ourselves by it and blame ourselves when we fall short.[50] It is sobering to consider the extent to which the Victorian ideal of woman as "angel in the house" has survived even into the era of so-called postfeminism. The dispensing of "female tenderness"—by no means coupled with "unadulterated power"—is still seen, even by writers who declare themselves sympathetic to the aims of the women's movement, as crucial to the manifestation and enactment of femininity.

In regard to the dispensing of female tenderness, the claims of feminist theorists such as Ferguson have been vindicated.[51] Women run real risks of exploitation in the transactions of heterosexual caregiving, indeed, of exploitation in the Marxist sense that Ferguson intends. All too frequently, women's caregiving involves an unequal exchange in which one party to this exchange is disempowered by the particular inequalities that characterize the exchange itself. This disempowerment, I have argued, lies in women's active and affective assimilation of the world according to men; it lies too in certain satisfactions of caregiving that serve to mystify our situation still further. Such disempowerment, like the disempowerment of the wage worker, may be described as a species of alienation, i.e., as a prohibition on the development and exercise of capacities, the exercise of which is thought essential to a fully human existence (see Chapter 3). The capacity most at risk here is not, as in the traditional Marxist theory of alienation, the capacity for creative labor; rather, it is the capacity, free from the subtle manipulation of consent, to construct an ethical and epistemic standpoint of one's own. Hence, Marxist categories of analysis—categories that have to do with exploitation, alienation, and the organization of the labor process—are by no means irrelevant to women's experience or, as some postmodernist feminists have maintained, do they invariably distort the nature of this experience.[52] Quite the contrary: Marxist questions, if we know how to follow out their answers, can lead us into the heart of female subjectivity.

Many feminist theorists have characterized this disempowerment in metaphors of filling and emptying: Women fill men with their energies, thereby strengthening them and depleting ourselves. I have argued not that there is no depletion, but that this depletion is to be measured not only in an increase of male energies, or—as the safety-valve theory maintains—in a reduction in male tensions, but in subtle affective and ideational changes in women ourselves that, taken *in toto,* tend to keep us in a position of subservience.

Conservatives argue, in essence,that women's caregiving may be properly exchanged for men's economic support. This view is not defensible. The classic bargain so lauded by conservatives—economic support in return for domestic and emotional labor—has broken down under the weight of economic necessity. Many millions of women must work outside the home. The continuing need of these women for men's economic patronage is a measure of the undervaluation of women's labor in the waged sector. To their superexploitation at work is added a disproportionate share of domestic labor, childcare, and emotional labor; women in this situation are quadruply exploited. Nor should we forget the growing number of single women, some single mothers as well, who give emotional support to men in relationships of shorter or longer duration, but receive absolutely no economic recompense at all. But even in the dwindling number of cases in which men are willing and able to offer economic patronage to women, it would be difficult to show how such support could compensate a woman for the epistemic decentering, ethical damage, and general mystification that put us at risk in unreciprocated caregiving.

Recently, conservatives have been joined by a number of feminist theorists in the celebration of female nurturance. The motives of these thinkers differ: Conservatives extol traditional female virtues in the context of a larger defense of the sexual *status quo;* feminist theorists, especially those who are drawn to the idea of an "ethics of care" based on women's traditional nurturant activities, want to raise women's status by properly valuing our emotional work and to see this quality of caring extended to the formal domains of commerce and politics. I applaud these aims. However, many feminist thinkers who extol women's nurturance, like most conservatives, have just ignored the possibility that women may suffer moral damage in the doing of emotional labor.[53] Clearly, the development of any ethics of care needs to be augmented by a careful analysis of the pitfalls and temptations of caregiving itself.

It may be true as feminist object relations theorists claim, that in the course of individuation, women have less need than men to sever our primary attachment to the maternal caretaker; this may account for our more "permeable" ego-boundaries and the relatively greater importance of attachment and relationship in our lives. But this is only part of the story. The exigencies of female psychological development alone are not responsible for our greater propensity to offer succor and support. Feminist object-relations theory, like a feminist ethics of care, stands in need of an analysis of the subjective effects of the labor we perform on a daily basis—including our emotional labor—and of the ways in which this labor structures the subjectivity both of those who perform it and of those whom it serves.

Female subjectivity is constructed through a continuous process, a personal "engagement in the practices, discourses, and institutions that lend significance (value, meaning, and affect) to the events of the world"[54]: A case in point is the discourse and practice of caregiving in heterosexual intimacy and the institution of domesticity (or its equivalent) that contains it. Insofar as we want to change ourselves and our lives, it is far easier to imagine, indeed, to enact changes in the way we accord status and in the kind of labor we perform on a daily basis than to undertake the restructuring of our basic patterns of psychological response. I am not suggesting that such a restructuring is impossible or that we should not support radical changes in the organization of early infant care, such as coparenting, that might help to develop similar patterns of relationality in men and women.[55] My point is a familiar one: In order to develop an effective politics of everyday life, we need to understand better than we do now not only the processes of personality development, but the "micropolitics" of our most ordinary transactions, the ways in which we inscribe and reinscribe our subjection in the fabric of the ordinary. The most prominent features and many of the subjective effects of this inscription can be grasped independently of any particular theory of personality formation. We need to locate our subordination not only in the hidden recesses of the psyche but in the duties we are happy to perform and in what we thought were the innocent pleasures of everyday life.

Notes

Introduction

1. *The Basic Works of Aristotle,* ed. Richard McKeon (New York: Random House, 1941), 1094b, p.936.

2. *The Dialogues of Plato,* trans. M. A. Jowett (New York: Random House, 1937), *Republic* 486a, p. 746.

1 Toward a Phenomenology of Feminist Consciousness

Since the first publication of this paper, a number of studies have appeared that examine in some detail the varieties of feminism I mention at the beginning. Alison Jaggar's classic *Feminist Politics and Human Nature* (Totowa, N.J.: Rowman and Allanheld, 1983) offers a fine philosophical reconstruction and critique of the varieties of feminist theory; in addition, Jaggar offers both a philosophically sophisticated version of what has come to be called "socialist feminism," a tendency in feminist theory that incorporates themes from both Marxist and radical feminism. Rosemarie Tong, in *Feminist Thought: A Comprehensive Introduction* (Boulder, Colo.: Westview Press, 1989), discusses feminisms I do not mention, namely, existentialist, psychoanalytic, and postmodern feminism; the latter two are theoretical tendencies that have flowered since the publication of the paper. I recommend also Josephine Donovan, *Feminist Theory: The Intellectual Traditions of American Feminism* (New York: Ungar, 1985).

Excellent discussions of the larger transformations in American society that paved the way for the emergence of Second Wave feminism can be found in Jo Freeman, *Politics of Women's Liberation: A Case Study of an Emerging Social Movement and Its Relation to the Policy Process* (New York and London:

Longman, 1975), and in Myra Marx Ferree and Beth B. Hess, *Controversy and Coalition: The New Feminist Movement* (Boston: Twayne, 1985). For a discussion of the role of women in the civil rights movement, see Sara Evans, *Personal Politics: The Roots of Women's Liberation in the Civil Rights Movement and the New Left* (New York: Random House, 1979).

1. Robin Morgan, "Introduction: The Women's Revolution," in *Sisterhood Is Powerful* (New York: Random House, 1970), p.xiv. In what follows, the consciousness I discuss is the consciousness of a feminist who is female. The modes of awareness of men who are feminists, whatever they may be, I do not discuss.

2. By "social reality" I mean the ensemble of formal and informal relationships with other people in which we are now enmeshed or in which we are likely to become enmeshed, together with the attitudes, values, types of communication, and conventions which accompany such relationships. "Social reality" is the social life-world, the social environment as it is present to my consciousness.

3. Karl Marx, *A Contribution to the Critique of Political Economy* (Chicago: Charles H. Kerr, 1904), pp. 11–12.

4. See, however, Margaret Benston, "The Political Economy of Women's Liberation," *Monthly Review,* Vol. 21, No. 4; also Valerie K. Oppenheimer, *The Female Labor Force in the United States: Demographic and Economic Factors Governing Its Growth and Changing Composition* (Berkeley: University of California Press, 1970). Highly recommended also is the special issue, "The Political Economy of Women," of the *Review of Radical Political Economics,* Vol. 4, July 1972.

5. See Betty Friedan, *The Feminine Mystique* (New York: W. W. Norton, 1963).

6. For an interpretation of the student movement as a protest against the direction taken by capitalist society in its latest phase, see Herbert Gintis, "The New Working Class and Revolutionary Youth," *Socialist Revolution,* May–June 1970.

7. Jean-Paul Sartre, *Being and Nothingness,* translated by Hazel E. Barnes (New York: Philosophical Library, 1956), p. 531.

2 On Psychological Oppression

Several works that have appeared since the publication of this paper may interest the reader. Linda Tschirhart Sanford and Mary Ellen Donovan have written a lucid, detailed, and powerful account of the many sources of women's low self-esteem: *Women and Self-Esteem* (New York: Doubleday, 1984). Also recommended is Ann Wilson Schaef, *Women's Reality* (New York: Harper and Row, 1981). In *Common Differences: Conflicts in Black and White Feminist Perspectives* (New York: Anchor/Doubleday, 1981), Gloria Joseph and Jill Lewis examine differences, including psychological differences, between black and white women. Linda LeMoncheck has written an analytically acute monograph on the subject of sexual objectification, *Dehumanizing Women: Treating Persons as Sex Objects* (Totowa, N.J.: Rowman and Allanheld, 1985); she subjects my own view of sexual objectification to an extended discussion and critique. The exclusion of women in our society from cultural production, especially from art, literature, and music, has, of course, never been total. But since I wrote this paper, there has been an enormous outpouring of work in these fields by creative women seeking very self-consciously to express a female and often a feminist perspective. Some of this work has reached a mass audience, for example, the art of Judy Chicago, the music of Holly Near and Tracey Chapman, and the novels of Toni Morrison, Marilyn French, Alice Walker, Marge Piercy, Erica Jong, and Gloria Naylor.

1. Frantz Fanon, *Black Skins, White Masks* (New York: Grove Press, 1967), p.12.

2. Ibid.

3. For an excellent comparison of the concepts of exploitation and oppression, see Judith Farr Tormey, "Exploitation, Oppression and Self-Sacrifice," in *Women and Philosophy,* ed. Carol C. Gould and Marx W. Wartofsky (New York: G. P. Putnam's Sons, 1976), pp. 206–221.

4. Joyce Mitchell Cook, paper delivered at Philosophy and the Black Liberation Struggle Conference, University of Illinois, Chicago Circle, November 19–20, 1970.

5. Fanon's phenomenology of oppression, however, is almost entirely a phenomenology of the oppression of colonized *men.* He seems unaware of the ways in which the oppression of women by their men in the societies he examines is itself similar to the colonization of natives by Europeans. Sometimes, as in *A Dying Colonialism* (New York: Grove Press, 1968), he goes so far as to defend the clinging to oppressive practices, such as the sequestration of women in Moslem countries, as an authentic resistance by indigenous people to Western cultural intrusion. For a penetrating critique of Fanon's attitude toward women, see Barbara Burris, "Fourth World Manifesto," in *Radical Feminism,* ed. A. Koedt, E. Levine, and A. Rapone (New York: Quadrangle, 1973), pp. 322–357.

6. I have in mind Abraham Maslow's concept of autonomy, a notion which has the advantage of being neutral as regards the controversy between free will and determinism. For Maslow, the sources of behavior of autonomous or "psychologically free" individuals are more internal than reactive:

> Such people become far more self-sufficient and self-contained. The determinants which govern them are now primarily inner ones . . . . They are the laws of their own inner nature, their potentialities and capacities, their talents, their latent resources, their creative impulses, their needs to know themselves and to become more and more integrated and unified, more and more aware of what they really are, of what they really want, of what their call or vocation or fate is to be. *Toward a Psychology of Being,* 2d ed. [New York: D. Van Nostrand Co., 1968], p. 35).

It would be absurd to suggest that most men are autonomous in this sense of the term. Nevertheless, insofar as there are individuals who resemble this portrait, I think it likelier that they will be men than women—at least white women. I think it likely that more white men than white women *believe* themselves to be autonomous; this belief, even if false, is widely held, and this in itself has implications that are important to consider. Whatever the facts may be in regard to men's lives, the point to remember is this: women have been thought to have neither the capacity nor the right to aspire to an ideal of autonomy, an ideal to which there accrues, whatever its relation to mental health, an enormous social prestige.

7. Many feminists would object vigorously to my claim that there has been no female culture (see, e.g., Burris, "Fourth World Manifesto"). I am not claiming that women have had no enclaves within the dominant culture, that we have never made valuable contributions to the larger culture, or even that we have never dominated any avenue of cultural expression—one would have to think only of the way in which women have dominated certain forms of folk art (e.g., quilting). What I am claiming is that none of this adds up to a "culture," in the sense in which we speak of Jewish culture, Arapesh culture, or Afro-American culture. Further, the fact that many women are today engaged in the self-conscious attempt to create a female culture testifies, I think, to the situation regarding culture being essentially as I describe it.

8. The best-known modern theory of this type is, of course, Freud's. He maintains that the relative absence of women from the higher culture is the consequence of a lesser ability to sublimate libidinal drives. See "Femininity" in *New Introductory Lectures in Psychoanalysis* (New York: W. W. Norton, 1933).

9. I take it that something like this forms the backdrop to the enjoyment of the average movie. It is daunting to consider the magnitude of the task of neutralization or transformation of hostile cultural messages that must fall constantly to the average female, non-white or even working class white male TV watcher or moviegoer. The pleasure we continue to take in cultural products that may disparage us remains, at least to me something of a mystery.

10. There might be some objection to regarding ordinary sexual relations as involving sexual objectification, since this use of the term seems not to jibe with its use in more ordinary contexts. For Hegel, Marx, and Sartre, "objectification" is an important moment in the dialectic of consciousness. My decision to treat ordinary sexual relations or even sexual desire alone as involving some objectification is based on a desire to remain within this tradition. Further, Sartre's phenomenology of sexual desire in *Being and Nothingness* (New York: Philosophical Library, 1966) draws heavily on a concept of objectification in an unusually compelling description of the experienced character of that state:

> The caress by realizing the Other's incarnation reveals to me my own incarnation; that is, I make myself flesh in order to impel the Other to realize for-herself and for-me her own flesh, and my caresses cause my flesh to be born for me in so far as it is for the Other flesh causing her to be born as flesh. I make her enjoy my flesh through her flesh in order to compel her to feel herself flesh. And so possession truly appears as a double reciprocal incarnation. (p. 508)

What I call "objectification," Sartre here calls "incarnation," a refinement not necessary for my purposes. What he calls "sadism" is incarnation without reciprocity. Most of my examples of sexual objectification would fall into the latter category.

11. Fanon, *Black Skin, White Masks,* p. 177. Eldridge Cleaver sounds a similar theme in *Soul on Ice* (New York: Dell, 1968). The archetypal white man in American society, for Cleaver, is the "Omnipotent Administrator," the archetypal black man the "Super-Masculine Menial."

12. P. 180.

13. Erik Erikson, "Inner and Outer Space: Reflections on Womanhood," *Daedalus,* Vol. 93, 1961, pp. 582–606.

14. Mihailo Markovic, "Women's Liberation and Human Emancipation," in *Women and Philosophy,* pp. 165–166. In spite of this lapse and some questionable opinions concerning the nature of female sexuality, Markovic's paper is a most compelling defense of the claim that the emancipation of women cannot come about under capitalism.

15. Exod. 1:13–14.

16. The available clinical literature on the psychological effects of social inferiority supports this claim. See William H. Grier and Price M. Cobbs, *Black Rage* (New York: Grosset & Dunlap, 1969); Pauline Bart, "Depression in Middle-Aged Women," in *Women in Sexist Society,* ed. Vivian Gornick and Barbara Moran (New York: New American Library, 1971), pp. 163–186; also Phyllis Chesler, *Women and Madness* (New York: Doubleday, 1972).

17. Bertell Ollman, *Alienation: Marx's Conception of Man in Capitalist Society* (London and New York: Cambridge University Press, 1971), p. 135.

18. Ibid. p. 143.

19. Karl Marx, *The Economic and Philosophical Manuscripts of 1844,* ed. Dirk J. Struik (New York: International Publishers, 1964), p. 111.

20. Ibid.

21. The use of the masculine possessive pronoun is deliberate.

3 Narcissism, Femininity, and Alienation

1. "How to Look Your Best All Your Life," *McCall's,* July 1979, p. 18.

2. In Lydia Sargent, ed., *Women and Revolution* (Boston: South End Press, 1981).

3. See the influential anthology *Capitalist Patriarchy and the Case for Socialist Feminism,* edited by Zillah R. Eisenstein (New York and London: Monthly Review Press, 1979).

4. Alison Jaggar, *Feminist Politics and Human Nature* (Totowa, N.J.: Rowman and Allanheld, 1983).

5. See, e.g., Nancy Chodorow, *The Reproduction of Mothering* (Berkeley: University of California Press, 1978).

6. See, e.g., Eisenstein, op. cit.; Bridges and Hartmann, op. cit.; Annette Kuhn and Ann Marie Wolpe, eds., *Feminism and Materialism* (London: Routledge and Kegan Paul, 1978); Christine Delphy, *The Main Enemy: A Materialist Analysis of Women's Oppression* (London: Women's Resource and Research Centre Publications, 1977); Jane Flax, "Do Feminists Need Marxism?" *Quest*, Vol. III, No. 1, Summer 1976; also "A Materialist Theory of Women's Status," *Psychology of Women Quarterly*, Fall 1981; Gayle Rubin, "The Traffic in Women," in *Toward an Anthropology of Women*, ed. Rayna Reiter (New York: Monthly Review Press, 1975); Ann Ferguson, "Women as a Revolutionary Class in the U.S.," in *Between Labor and Capital*, ed. Pat Walker (Boston: South End Press, 1979); Sandra Harding, "What Is the Real Material Base of Patriarchy and Capital?" in Sargent, op. cit.; Nancy Hartsock, "The Feminist Standpoint: Developing the Ground for a Specifically Feminist Historical Materialism," in *Discovering Reality: Feminist Perspectives on Epistemology, Metaphysics, Methodology and the Philosophy of Science,* Sandra Harding and Merrill Hintikka, eds. (Dordrecht: Reidel Publishing Co. 1983), Susan Rae Peterson, "Feminism, Marxism and Reproduction," paper read to the Society for Women in Philosophy, Eastern Division APA, December 1980.

   For two critiques of some lines of argument laid out in the above, see Iris Young, "Socialist Feminism and the Limits of Dual Systems Theory," *Socialist Review,* March–June 1980; and Martha Gimenez, "The Oppression of Women: A Structuralist Marxist View," in Ino Rossi, ed., *Structural Sociology: Theoretical Perspectives and Substantive Analysis* (New York: Columbia University Press, 1982).

7. Karl Marx, "Estranged Labor" in *The Economic and Philosophic Manuscripts of 1844* (New York: International Publishers, 1964), p. 110.

8. For a fuller discussion, see Bertell Ollman, *Alienation: Marx's Conception of Man in Capitalist Society* (London: Cambridge University Press, 1971).

9. Iris Young, "Is There a Woman's World?—Some Reflections on the Struggle for Our Bodies," a lecture presented to The Second Sex—Thirty Years Later: A Commemorative Conference on Feminist Theory, sponsored by the New York Institute for the Humanities, New York University, September 1979; see also her "Throwing Like a Girl: A Phenomenology of Feminine Body Comportment, Motility and Spatiality," *Human Studies*, Vol. 3, 1980, pp. 137–156.

10. For a fuller examination of sexual objectification see the previous chapter.

11. Sigmund Freud, "On Narcissism: An Introduction," in *General Selection from the Works of Sigmund Freud* (New York: Doubleday/Anchor, 1957), p. 104.

12. My use of the term also conforms to Beauvoir's usage; I discuss her work below. The term *narcissism* has been used to refer to a normal stage of infantile development, a form of sexual perversion, a type of personality disorder seen with increasing frequency by contemporary clinicians (Kohutt and Kernberg), and, most recently, the values and style of late capitalist culture (Lasch). For a trenchant critique of the latter view, see Stephanie Engel, "Femininity as Tragedy: Reexamining the New Narcissism," *Socialist Review,* Sept.–Oct. 1980.

13. Sigmund Freud, "Instincts and their Vicissitudes," *General Selection,* p. 81.

14. Freud, "The Psychology of Women," chapter 23, in *New Introductory Lectures on Psychoanalysis* (London: Hogarth Press, 1933). Penis envy is at the root of the "greater amount of narcissism attributed by psychoanalysis to women. . . . their vanity is partly a further effect of penis-envy, for they are driven to rate their physical charms more highly as a belated compensation for their original sexual inferiority" (p. 160).

15. Freud, "On Narcissism," *General Selection,* p. 112–113.

16. Helene Deutsch, *Psychology of Women,* Vol. I (New York: Grune and Stratton, 1944), p. 105.

17. Simone de Beauvoir, *The Second Sex* (New York: Bantam Books, 1961), p. 300.

18. Ibid., p. 316.

19. Ibid., p. 375.

20. Ibid., p. 508.

21. Freud, "On Narcissism," *General Selection,* p. 111.

22. See Susan Sontag's superb treatment of the subject of women and aging, "The Double Standard of Aging," in Juanita H. Williams, ed., *Psychology of Women: Selected Readings* (New York: W. W. Norton, 1979), pp. 462–478.

23. Quoted in "Fashion, Beauty and the Feminist," *The Freewoman,* Sept.–Oct. 1978, p. 1.

24. See Phyllis Chesler and Emily Jane Goodman, *Women, Money and Power* (New York: Morrow, 1976), pp. 47–48. These images are not only unattainable but often incompatible as well. Thus, in the same magazine, for example, women may be encouraged to look mysterious and seductive on one page, apple-cheeked and virginal on the next.

25. While the fashion-beauty complex produces fears about the acceptability of the body, at the same time it feeds anxieties generated elsewhere. Two examples will suffice: first, the relatively recent entry of millions of women into a sex-segregated labor market where they must compete with other women often on the basis of appearance; second, a growing divorce rate which in effect denies tenure in marriage and which tends to disadvantage women relative to men in the older age ranges.

26. Herbert Marcuse, *One-Dimensional Man* (Boston: Beacon Press, 1964), p. 7.

27. We should not forget that the original women's liberation demonstration of the feminist second wave was a burlesque of the Miss America Pageant in Atlantic City.

4 Feminine Masochism and the Politics of Personal Transformation

1. Alison Jaggar, *Feminist Politics and Human Nature* (Totowa, N.J.: Rowman and Allanheld, 1983), p. 122.

2. *Ms.,* July–August 1982, p. 35.

3. Maria Marcus, *A Taste for Pain: On Masochism and Female Sexuality* (New York: St. Martin's Press, 1981), p. 46. Needless to say, the having of a fantasy, every

detail of which the woman orchestrates herself, is not like a desire for actual rape. The pervasive fear of rape hangs like a blight over the lives of women, where it may severely restrict spontaneity and freedom of movement. Even if a woman escapes impregnation, venereal disease, or grave bodily injury during a rape, the psychological consequences to her may be devastating. The aftermath of rape, only recently documented by feminist scholars, may include nightmares, excessive fearfulness, phobic behavior, loss of sexual desire, and the erosion of intimate relationships. None of this is part of the typical rape fantasy.

4. A recent history of women in Hollywood film sets out at some length the increasingly brutal treatment of women in the movies, movies made by men to be sure, but patronized and enjoyed by large numbers of women. See Molly Haskell, *From Reverence to Rape* (New York: Penguin Books, 1974).

5. Sara Craven, *Moth to the Flame* (Toronto: Harlequin Books, 1979).

6. Beatrice Faust, *Women, Sex and Pornography* (New York: Macmillan, 1980), p. 147. "Sweet Savagery girls cede a great deal of the responsibility to the heroes, saying no until virile and sometimes vicious men force them to say yes. Much of the time the relationship between heroines and heroes is that of master and slave, teacher and pupil, leader and the led. The heroines achieve autonomy only to relinquish it in marriage." Ibid., p. 156.

7. For a penetrating analysis of the Harlequin-type romance, see Ann Barr Snitow, "Mass Market Romance: Pornography for Women Is Different," *Radical History Review*, Vol. 20, Spring-Summer, 1979), pp. 141–161.

8. John Deigh, "Shame and Self-Esteem: A Critique," *Ethics*, Vol. 93, January 1983, pp. 225–245.

9. Laura Lederer, ed., *Take Back the Night: Women on Pornography* (New York: William Morrow, 1980).

10. Janet Schrim, "A Proud and Emotional Statement," in Samois, ed., *What Color Is Your Handkerchief?* (Berkeley, Calif.: Samois, 1979), p. 24.

11. Pat Califia, "Feminism and Sadomasochism," *Heresies*, Vol. 12, p. 32.

12. Martha Equinox, "If I Ask You to Tie Me Up, Will You Still Want to Love Me?" in Samois, ed., *Coming to Power* (Berkeley, Calif.: Samois, 1981), p. 36; also Susan Farr, "The Art of Discipline: Creating Erotic Dramas of Play and Power," Ibid., p. 187.

13. Gayle Rubin, "The Leather Menace: Comments on Politics and S/M," in *Coming to Power*, pp. 211 and 193.

14. For another analysis of Samois's position and an attack on lesbian sadomasochism, see Bat-Ami Bar-On, "Feminism and Sadomasochism: Self-Critical Notes," in Linden et. al., *Against Sadomasochism: A Radical Feminist Analysis* (Palo Alto, Calif.: Frog-in-the-Well Press, 1982); also, in the same volume, Sarah Lucia Hoagland, "Sadism, Masochism and Lesbian-Feminism."

15. Gayle Rubin, "The Traffic in Women," in Rayna Reiter, ed., *Toward an Anthropology of Women* (New York: Monthly Review Press, 1975), p. 161.

16. "I believe that freedom for women must begin in the repudiation of our own

masochism . . . . I believe that ridding ourselves of our own deeply entrenched masochism, which takes so many tortured forms, is the first priority: it is the first deadly blow that we can strike against systematized male dominance.'' Andrea Dworkin, *Our Blood: Prophecies and Discourses on Sexual Politics* (New York: Perigee Books, 1976), p. 111.

17. This receives confirmation from a contemporary feminist psychologist: "Masochistic and hysterical behavior is so similar to the concept of 'femininity' that the three are not clearly distinguishable." Betsy Belote, "Masochistic Syndrome, Hysterical Personality and the Illusion of a Healthy Woman," in Sue Cox, ed., *Female Psychology: The Emerging Self* (Chicago: Science Research Associates, 1976), p. 347.

18. Sigmund Freud, "The Psychology of Women," Chapter 23 of *New Introductory Lectures on Psychoanalysis* (London: Hogarth Press, 1933).

19. Helene Deutsch, "Significance of Masochism in the Mental Life of Women," *Int. J. Psychoanalysis,* 11, (1930) pp. 48–60; also, *Psychology of Women* (New York: Grune and Stratton, 1944).

20. Cited in Janine Chasseguet-Smirgel, *Female Sexuality: New Psychoanalytic Views* (London: Virago Press, 1981), p. 29.

21. Belote, op. cit., p. 337.

22. Sandor Rado, *Psychoanalysis of Behavior* (New York: Grune and Stratton, 1956).

23. See, for example, Marcus, op. cit.

24. Cited in Chasseguet-Smirgel, op. cit., p. 13.

25. Theodore Reik, *Masochism in Sex and Society* (New York: Grove Press, 1962), p. 217. Freud makes a similar observation (see Chasseguet-Smirgel, p. 131).

26. Cited in Chasseguet-Smirgel, op. cit. p. 97.

27. Helle Thorning, "The Mother-Daughter Relationship and Sexual Ambivalence," *Heresies,* Vol. 12, 1981, pp. 23–26. For a more complex development of a similar theory, see Jessica Benjamin, "The Bonds of Love: Rational Violence and Erotic Domination," *Feminist Studies,* Vol. 6, No. 1, pp. 144–174. Thorning and Benjamin make use of accounts within object-relations theory of pre-Oedipal development, especially of the genesis of male and female gender-personality in relation to the maternal caregiver; for the most influential such account within feminist theory, see Nancy Chodorow, *The Reproduction of Mothering: Psychoanalysis and the Sociology of Gender* (Berkeley, Calif.: University of California Press, 1978).

28. See George Bataille, *Death and Sensuality* (New York: Walker and Co., 1962); also Jean-Paul Sartre, *Being and Nothingness* (New York: Philosophical Library, 1956), esp. Part 3, Chapter 3, "Concrete Relations with Others," pp. 361–430.

29. See H. J. Eysenck, "The Effects of Psychotherapy: An Evaluation," *Journal of Consulting Psychology,* Vol. 16, 1952, pp. 319–324. For further discussion of this topic, see A. J. Fix and E. Haffke, *Basic Psychological Therapies: Comparative Effectiveness* (New York: Human Sciences Press, 1976).

30. Linda Phelps, "Female Sexual Alienation," in Jo Freeman, ed., *Women: A Feminist Perspective,* 2d ed. (Palo Alto, Calif.: Mayfield, 1979).

31. See Sarah Lucia Hoagland, "Sadism, Masochism and Lesbian-Feminism," in *Against Sadomasochism.*

32. Jeannette Nichols, Darlene Pagano, and Margaret Rossoff, "Is Sadomasochism Feminist?" in *Against Sadomasochism.* Many feminists, especially those in the anti-pornography movement, believe that men in particular will want to imitate the images of sexual behavior with which they are now being bombarded; this accounts for the urgency of these feminists' attack on male-oriented violent pornography. See Laura Lederer, ed., *Take Back the Night,* esp. Ann Jones, "A Little Knowledge," pp. 179 and 183, and Diana E. H. Russell, "Pornography and Violence: What Does the New Research Say?" p. 236.

33. Ethel Spector Person, "Sexuality as the Mainstay of Identity: Psychoanalytic Perspectives," *Signs,* Vol. 5, No. 4, Summer 1980, pp. 605–630.

34. The literature of lesbian separatism, in particular, is replete with examples of sexual voluntarism: " 'Do what feels good. Sex is groovy. Gay is just as good as straight. I don't care what you do in bed, so you shouldn't care what I do in bed.' This argument assumes that Lesbians have the same lifestyle and sexuality as straight women. But we don't—straight women choose to love and fuck men. Lesbians have commitments to women. Lesbians are not born. We have made a conscious choice to be Lesbians. We have rejected all that is traditional and accepted, and committed ourselves to a lifestyle that everybody . . . criticizes." Barbara Solomon, "Taking the Bullshit by the Horns," in Nancy Myron and Charlotte Bunch, eds., *Lesbianism and the Women's Movement* (Baltimore: Diana Press, 1975), p. 40. For similar statements, see in the same volume, pp. 18, 36, and 70.

35. Ethel Spector Person, op. cit., p. 620.

36. Ibid., p. 620.

37. Ibid., p. 625.

38. Ibid., p. 627.

39. Robert Stoller, *Sexual Excitement* (New York: Simon and Schuster, 1979), pp. 6 and 13.

40. Person, op, cit., p. 621.

5 Foucault, Femininity, and the Modernization of Patriarchal Power

1. Michel Foucault, *Discipline and Punish* (New York: Vintage Books, 1979), p. 138.

2. Ibid., p. 28.

3. Ibid., p. 147.

4. Ibid., p. 153. Foucault is citing an eighteenth-century military manual, "Ordonnance du Ier janvier 1766 . . ., titre XI, article 2."

5. Ibid., p. 153.

6. Ibid., p. 150.

7. Ibid., p. 200.

8. Ibid., p. 201.

9. Ibid., p. 228.

10. Judith Butler, "Embodied Identity in De Beauvoir's *The Second Sex,*" unpublished manuscript, p. 11, presented to American Philosophical Association, Pacific Division, March 22, 1985. See also Butler's recent monograph *Gender Trouble: Feminism and the Subversion of Identity* (New York: Routledge, 1990).

11. Marcia Millman, *Such a Pretty Face-Being Fat in America* (New York: Norton, 1980), p. 46.

12. Susan Bordo, "Anorexia Nervosa: Psychopathology as the Crystallization of Culture," *Philosophical Forum,* Vol. XVII, No. 2, Winter 1985–86, pp. 73–104. See also Bordo's *Food, Fashion and Power: The Body and The Reproduction of Gender* (forthcoming, v. of California Press).

13. *USA Today,* May 30, 1985.

14. Phrase taken from the title of Kim Chernin's *The Obsession: Reflections on the Tyranny of Slenderness* (New York: Harper and Row, 1981), an examination from a feminist perspective of women's eating disorders and of the current female preoccupation with body size.

15. M. J. Saffon, *The 15-Minute-A-Day Natural Face Lift* (New York: Warner Books, 1981).

16. Sophia Loren, *Women and Beauty* (New York: William Morrow, 1984), p. 57.

17. Iris Young, "Throwing Like a Girl: A Phenomenology of Feminine Body Comportment, Motility and Spatiality," *Human Studies,* Vol. 3, (1980), pp. 137–156.

18. Marianne Wex, *Let's Take Back Our Space: "Female" and "Male" Body Language as a Result of Patriarchal Structures* (Berlin: Frauenliteraturverlag Hermine Fees, 1979). Wex claims that Japanese women are still taught to position their feet so that the toes point inward, a traditional sign of submissiveness (p. 23).

19. In heels, the "female foot and leg are turned into ornamental objects and the impractical shoe, which offers little protection against dust, rain and snow, induces helplessness and dependence. . . . The extra wiggle in the hips, exaggerating a slight natural tendency, is seen as sexually flirtatious while the smaller steps and tentative, insecure tread suggest daintiness, modesty and refinement. Finally, the overall hobbling effect with its sadomasochistic tinge is suggestive of the restraining leg irons and ankle chains endured by captive animals, prisoners and slaves who were also festooned with decorative symbols of their bondage." Susan Brownmiller, *Femininity* (New York: Simon and Schuster, 1984), p. 184.

20. Nancy Henley, *Body Politics* (Englewood Cliffs, N. J.: Prentice-Hall, 1977), p. 176.

21. For an account of the sometimes devastating effects on workers, like flight attendants, whose conditions of employment require the display of a perpetual friendliness, see Arlie Hochschild, *The Managed Heart: The Commercialization of Human Feeling* (Berkeley, Calif.: University of California Press, 1983).

22. Henley, *Body Politics,* p. 108.

23. Ibid., p. 149.

24. Clairol has just introduced a small electric shaver, the "Bikini," apparently intended for just such use.

25. Georgette Klinger and Barbara Rowes, *Georgette Klinger's Skincare* (New York: William Morrow, 1978, pp. 102, 105, 151, 188, and passim.

26. *Chicago Magazine,* March 1986, pp. 43, 10, 18, and 62.

27. *Essence,* April 1986, p. 25. I am indebted to Laurie Shrage for calling this to my attention and for providing most of these examples.

28. Klinger, *Skincare,* pp. 137–140.

29. In light of this, one is surprised to see a two-ounce jar of "Skin Regeneration Formula," a "Proteolytic Enzyme Cream with Bromelain and Papain," selling for $23.95 in the tabloid *Globe* (April 8, 1986, p. 29) and an unidentified amount of Tova Borgnine's "amazing new formula from Beverly Hills" (otherwise unnamed) going for $41.75 in the *National Enquirer* (April 8, 1986, p. 15).

30. "It is required of woman that in order to realize her femininity she must make herself object and prey, which is to say that she must renounce her claims as sovereign subject." *Simone De Beauvoir, The Second Sex* (New York: Bantam Books, 1968), p. 642.

31. The film *Pumping Iron II* portrays very clearly the tension for female bodybuilders (a tension that enters into formal judging in the sport) between muscular development and a properly feminine appearance.

32. Henley, *Body Politics,* p. 101, 153, and passim.

33. Foucault, *Discipline and Punish,* p. 222.

34. Millman, *Such a Pretty Face,* p. 80. These sorts of remarks are made so commonly to heavy women that sociologist Millman takes the most clichéd as title of her study of the lives of the overweight.

35. I am indebted to Nancy Fraser for the formulation of this point.

36. See Chapter 3.

37. Millman, *Such a Pretty Face,* pp. 80 and 195.

38. Chernin, *The Obsession,* p. 53.

39. See Chapter 3.

40. For a claim that the project of liberal or "mainstream" feminism is covertly racist, see Bell Hooks, *Ain't I Woman: Black Women and Feminism* (Boston: South End Press, 1981), Chap. 4. For an authoritative general critique of liberal feminism, see Alison Jaggar, *Feminist Politics and Human Nature* (Totowa, N. J.: Rowman and Allanheld, 1983), Chaps. 3 and 7.

41. See, for example, Mihailo Markovic, "Women's Liberation and Human Emancipation," in *Women and Philosophy,* ed. Carol C. Gould and Marx W. Wartofsky (New York: G. P. Putnam's Sons, 1976), pp. 165–166.

42. Foucault, *Discipline and Punish,* p. 30.

43. Some radical feminists have called for just such a deconstruction. See especially

Monique Wittig, *The Lesbian Body* (New York: Avon Books, 1976), and Butler, *Gender Trouble.*

44. Foucault, *Discipline and Punish,* p. 44.

45. Foucault, Colin Gordon, ed., *Power/Knowledge* (Brighton, 1980), p. 151. Quoted in Peter Dews, "Power and Subjectivity in Foucault," *New Left Review,* No. 144, March–April 1984, p. 17.

46. Dews, op. cit., p. 77.

47. Foucault, *Discipline and Punish,* p. 138.

48. Ibid., p. 201.

49. Foucault, *Power/Knowledge,* p. 98. In fact, Foucault is not entirely consistent on this point. For an excellent discussion of contending Foucault interpretations and for the difficulty of deriving a consistent set of claims from Foucault's work generally, see Nancy Fraser, "Michel Foucault: A 'Young Conservative'?" *Ethics,* Vol. 9(?) October 1985, pp. 165–184.

50. Dews, op. cit., p. 92.

51. See Marcia Hutchinson, *Transforming Body Image-Learning to Love the Body You Have* (Trumansburg, N.Y.: Crossing Press, 1985). See also Bordo, "Anorexia Nervosa: Psychopathology as the Crystallization of Culture."

6 Shame and Gender

1. See for example, Anthony Kenny, *Action, Emotion and the Will* (London: Routledge & Kegan Paul, 1963); J. R. S. Wilson, *Emotion and Object* (Cambridge: Cambridge University Press, 1972); R. M. Gordon, "Aboutness of Emotion," *American Philosophical Quarterly,* Vol. XI, No. 1, Jan. 1974; Robert Solomon, "The Logic of Emotion," *Nous,* Vol. XI, No. 1, 1977, and *The Passions* (New York: Doubleday, 1976); Irving Thalberg, "Emotion and Thought," *American Philosophical Quarterly,* Vol. 1, 1964, and *Perception, Emotion and Action* (Oxford: Basil Blackwell, 1977); Donald Davidson, "Hume's Cognitive Theory of Pride," *Journal of Philosophy,* Vol. LXXIII, No. 19, Nov. 1976; Gabriele Taylor, *Pride, Shame and Guilt: Emotions of Self-Assessment* (Oxford: Oxford University Press, 1985).

2. Martin Heidegger, *Being and Time,* trans. Macquarrie and Robinson (New York: Harper and Row, 1962), p. 173. See Section 29, "Being-there as State-of-mind," pp. 172–179.

3. Ibid., p. 177. Michael Stocker has been one of the few Anglo-American philosophers to explore the relationship between intellect and patterns of choice, desire, and emotion. See his "Intellectual Desire, Emotion and Action," in Amelie Oksenberg Rorty, ed., *Explaining Emotions* (Berkeley: University of California Press, 1980).

4. See, for example, Evelyn Fox Keller, *Reflections on Gender and Science* (New Haven: Yale University Press, 1985); Sandra Harding, *The Science Question in Feminism* (Ithaca: Cornell University Press, 1986); Susan Bordo, "The Cartesian

Masculinization of Thought," in Sandra Harding and Jean F. O'Barr, eds., *Sex and Scientific Inquiry* (Chicago: University of Chicago Press, 1987); Sandra Harding and Merrill Hintikka, eds., *Discovering Reality: Feminist Perspectives on Epistemology, Metaphysics, Methodology and Philosophy of Science* (Dordrecht: Reidel, 1983): Alison M. Jaggar, *Feminist Politics and Human Nature* (Totowa, N.J.: Rowman and Allanheld, 1983), esp. Chapter 11; Genevieve Lloyd, *The Man of Reason* (Minneapolis: University of Minnesota Press, 1984); Mary Belenky, Blythe Clinchy, Nancy Goldberger, and Jill Tarule, *Women's Ways of Knowing* (New York: Basic Books, 1986).

5. See, for example, Leslie R. Brody, "Gender Differences in Emotional Development: A Review of Theories and Research," in Abigail J. Stewart and M. Brenton Lykes, eds., *Gender and Personality: Current Perspectives on Theory and Research* (Durham: Duke University Press, 1985); also, Arlie Hochschild, *The Managed Heart* (Berkeley: University of California Press, 1983).

6. Husseen Abdilahi Bulhan, *Frantz Fanon and the Psychology of Oppression* (New York: Plenum Press, 1985), p. 122. Bulhan uses this phrase to characterize slaves and oppressed persons of color. Citing the work of psychologists Orlando Patterson and Chester Pierce, Bulhan characterizes a "generalized condition of dishonor" as a status in which one's person lacks integrity, worth and autonomy and in which one is subject to violations of space, time, energy, mobility, bonding and identity.

7. Susan Miller, *The Shame Experience* (Hillsdale, N.J.: The Analytic Press, 1985), p. 32.

8. Jean-Paul Sartre, *Being and Nothingness,* translated by Hazel E. Barnes (New York: Philosophical Library, 1956), p. 221–222.

9. Ibid., p. 222.

10. Ibid.

11. Ibid.

12. Arnold Isenberg, "Natural Pride and Natural Shame," in Rorty, op. cit., p. 366.

13. Taylor, op. cit., p. 61.

14. John Deigh, "Shame and Self-Esteem: A Critique," *Ethics,* Vol. 93, January 1983, p. 242.

15. Helen Merrell Lynd, *Shame and the Search for Identity* (New York: Harcourt Brace and Co., 1958), p. 46.

16. Ibid., p. 47.

17. John Rawls, *A Theory of Justice* (Cambridge: Harvard University Press, 1971), pp. 440–446.

18. Deigh, op. cit., p. 235.

19. Ibid.

20. Ibid.

21. Ibid., p. 241.

22. Ibid., p. 225.

23. Miller, op. cit., p. 3.

24. Some relevant studies are discussed in M. W. Matlin, *The Psychology of Women* (New York: Holt, Rinehart and Winston, 1987), pp. 129–132.

25. For discussions of "women's language," see Robin Lakoff, *Language and Women's Place* (New York: Harper and Row, 1975); Barrie Thorne and Nancy Henley, eds., *Language and Sex: Difference and Dominance.* (Rowley, Mass.: Newbury House Publishers, 1975); Nancy Henley, *Body Politics: Power, Sex and Non-Verbal Communication* (Englewood Cliffs, N.J.: Prentice-Hall, 1977).

26. Isenberg, op. cit., p. 370.

27. Roberta M. Hall, with the assistance of Bernice R. Sandler, "The Classroom Climate: A Chilly One for Women?" prepared by the Project on the Status and Education of Women of the Association of American Colleges, 1818 R St., N.W., Washington, D.C. 20009. The claims I make in this section about differences in treatment of male and female students are drawn almost entirely from empirical studies cited in the body of the report or in the notes and Selected List of Resources. See esp. pp. 17–21.

28. An excellent review and evaluation of this research can be found in Stephanie Riger and Pat Galligan, "Women in Management: An Exploration of Compeling Paradigms," *American Psychologist,* Vol. 35., No. 10, October 1980, pp. 902–910. Also See Pauline Rose Clance, *The Imposture Phenomenon* (New York: Bantam, 1985), also Pauline Rose Clance and Suzanne Jones, "The Imposture Phenomenon in High-Achieving Women: Dynamics and Therapeutic Intervention," *Psychotherapy: Theory, Research and Practice,* 1978, Vol. 15, pp. 241–247.

29. Classroom Climate, p. 8.

30. Taylor, op. cit., p. 2.

31. Ronald R. DeSousa, *The Rationality of Emotion* (Cambridge: MIT Press, 1987), p. 137.

32. Taylor, op. cit., p. 1. See also Davidson, op. cit.

33. Isenberg, op. cit., p. 368.

34. Taylor, op. cit., p. 140.

35. The use of masculine pronouns in this paragraph is, of course, deliberate.

36. Taylor, op. cit., p. 15.

37. Ibid., p. 141.

38. "Phenomenally, we would wholly fail to recognize both *what* mood discloses and *how* it discloses, if that which is disclosed were to be compared with what Dasein is acquainted with, knows and believes 'at the same time' when it has such a mood." Heidegger, op. cit., p. 175.

39. Rorty, op. cit., p. 120.

7 Feeding Egos and Tending Wounds

1. Shulamith Firestone, *The Dialectic of Sex* (New York: Bantam Books, 1971), p. 127.

2. Connell Cowan and Melvyn Kinder, *Smart Women, Foolish Choices* (New York: Signet, 1986), p. 229.

3. Ibid., p. 230.

4. Ibid., p. 73.

5. Ibid., p. 75.

6. Ibid., p. 150.

7. In addition to Kinder and Cowan, see for example, Nancy Good, *How to Love a Difficult Man* (New York: St. Martin's Press, 1987); Robin Norwood, *Women Who Love Too Much* (New York: Simon and Schuster/Pocket Books, 1986); Dr. Susan Forward and Joan Torres, *Men Who Hate Women and the Women Who Love Them* (New York: Bantam Books, 1986); Colette Dowling, *The Cinderella Complex: Woman's Hidden Fear of Independence* (New York: Simon and Schuster/Pocket Books, 1982).

8. Ann Ferguson, *Blood at the Root: Motherhood, Sexuality and Male Dominance* (London: Unwin Hyman, Pandora Press, 1989), Chapter 4. See also Ferguson's earlier essay "Women as a New Revolutionary Class in the U.S," in Pat Walker, ed., *Between Labor and Management* (Boston: South End Press, 1979), p. 18.

9. Ferguson, "Women as a New Revolutionary Class, p. 23; see also *Blood at the Root,* pp. 130–136.

10. Ibid., p. 133.

11. "Women as a New Revolutionary Class," pp. 20–21.

12. Joel Feinberg, *Harm to Others* (New York: Oxford University Press, 1984), p. 178.

13. Ibid., p. 194.

14. Ibid., p. 209.

15. For an excellent discussion of the connection in Marxist theory between unequal exchange and disempowerment, see Iris Young, "Five Faces of Oppression," *Philosophical Forum,* Vol. XIX, No. 4, Summer 1988, esp. p. 277.

16. An example of this kind of thinking can be found in Marabel Morgan, *The Total Woman* (Old Tappan, N.J: F. H. Revell, 1973).

17. Lillian Rubin, *Worlds of Pain: Life in the Working-Class Family* (New York: Basic Books, 1976).

18. Mirra Komarovsky, *Blue Collar Marriage* (New York: Random House, 1962).

19. Robert Staples, a noted sociologist of black sex roles, acknowledges that these attitudes are widespread among black men in "The Myth of Black Macho: A Response to Angry Black Feminists," in *The Black Scholar,* March–April 1979.

20. See for example the exchange in the *Black Scholar,* May–June 1979; also Bell Hooks, *Ain't I a Woman: Black Women and Feminism* (Boston: South End Press, 1981), esp. p. 79 and 181–187; and *Feminist Theory from Margin to Center* (Boston: South End Press, 1984).

21. See, e.g., Audre Lord, "The Great American Disease," in *The Black Scholar,* May–June 1979.

22. Arlie Hochschild, *The Managed Heart: The Commercialization of Human Feeling* (Berkeley, Calif.: University of California Press, 1983).

23. Ibid., p. 122.

24. Ibid., p. 7.

25. Ibid., p. 8.

26. Arlie Hochschild, "Smile Wars, Counting the Casualties of Emotional Labor," *Mother Jones,* December 1983, p. 40.

27. Hochschild, *The Managed Heart,* p. 131.

28. See e.g. Firestone, *op. cit;* Ti-Grace Atkinson, "Metaphysical Cannibalism" in *Amazon Odyssey* (N.Y.: Links Books, 1974, p. 53 and Marilyn Frye, *Politics of Reality* (Trumansburg, N.Y.: Crossing Press, 1983).

29. See Rosalind Coward, *Female Desires* (New York: Grove Press, 1983), p. 140; also Sheila Rowbotham, *Woman's Consciousness, Man's World* (Baltimore: Penguin Books, 1973) and *Politics of Sexuality in Capitalism* (London: Red Collective and Publications Distribution Cooperative, 1978), p. 46.

30. Lillian Rubin, *Just Friends* (New York: Harper and Row, 1985), p. 69.

31. Ibid., p. 90.

32. Ibid.

33. Jesse Bernard, "The Paradox of the Happy Marriage," in *Woman in Sexist Society,* ed. by Vivian Gornick and Barbara K. Moran (New York: Basic Books, 1971).

34. Theodore Kemper, *A Social Interactional Theory of Emotions* (New York: John Wiley and Sons, 1978), p. 285.

35. Ibid., p. 96. "Since giving and according status are, by definition , at the heart of love relationships and only one sex is particularly expected to be competent in the performance of this attribute—*although both sexes require it* if the mutuality of the relationship is to be maintained—it is likely that the deficit of affection and love given by men to women will have devastating effects on the relationship. Wives in troubled marriages do in fact report more often than their husbands a lack of demonstrated affection, tenderness and love. . . . This is precisely what we would have expected from an examination of the sex-linked differential in standards for status conferral that is an obvious feature of our culture." Kemper, *A Social Interactional Theory of Emotions,* p. 320.

36. See Hochschild, *The Managed Heart,* p. 168. See also Nancy Henley, *Body Politics* (New York: Simon and Schuster, 1977), esp. Chapters 6, 9, and 10.

37. Dorothy Dinnerstein, *The Mermaid and the Minotaur* (New York: Harper and Row, 1977) and Nancy Chodorow, *The Reproduction of Mothering: Psychoanalysis and the Sociology of Gender* (Berkeley: University of California Press, 1978).

38. Given the context, my use of masculine pronouns is deliberate.

39. Nel Noddings, *Caring: A Feminine Approach to Ethics and Moral Education* (Berkeley: University of California Press, 1984), pp. 14 and 30.

40. Ibid., p. 24.

41. See, for example, Mary Field Belenky, Blythe McVicker Clinchy, Nancy Rule Goldberger, and Jill Mattuck Garule, *Women's Ways of Knowing: The Development of Self, Voice and Mind* (New York: Basic Books, 1986).

42. Hegel, *The Phenomenology of Spirit,* trans. A. V. Miller (London: Oxford University Press, 1977), pp. 267–279; see also Judith M. Miles, *The Feminine Principle* (Minneapolis: Bethany Fellowship, 1975).

43. John Stuart Mill, "The Subjection of Women," in *Essays on Sex Equality,* ed. Alice S. Rossi (Chicago: University of Chicago Press, 1970).

44. Jill Tweedie, *In the Name of Love* (London: Jonathan Cape, 1979), p. 49.

45. Sara Ruddick, "Maternal Thinking," in *Women and Values: Readings in Recent Feminist Philosophy,* ed. Marilyn Pearsall (Belmont, Calif.: Wadsworth Publishing Co., 1986), p. 342.

46. William James, review of Horace Bucknell, *Women's Suffrage and Reform Against Nature* (New York: Scribner, 1869) and John Stuart Mill, *The Subjection of Women* (New York: Appleton, 1869), *North American Review,* October 1869, pp. 562–563. Cited in Linda A. Bell, "Does Marriage Require a Head? Some Historical Arguments," *Hypatia,* Vol. 4, No. 1, Spring 1989, p. 148.

47. I think that this may be true only for occasional or nonserious abuse. Women stay with chronic abusers either because of the serious emotional injury done them in long-term abusive situations—impairment of judgment, "learned helplessness," disablingly low self-esteem, or fear of worse abuse if they try to leave—or else for largely economic reasons. See Susan Schechter, *Women and Male Violence: The Struggles of the Battered Women's Movement* (Boston: South End Press, 1982).

48. Michel Foucault, *History of Sexuality,* Vol. I (New York: Random House/Vintage Books, 1980), pp. 58–62.

49. Nahum N. Glatzer, *The Loves of Franz Kafka* (New York: Schocken Books, 1986), p. x.

50. The risks to women will, of course, vary from one case to the next; they may be a function of a woman's age or her degree of economic or emotional dependency on the man or the presence or absence in her life of resources with which to construct a picture of the world according to herself.

51. See note 8 above.

52. See, for example, Jane Flax, "Postmodernism and Gender Relations in Feminist Theory," in Michelene R. Malson, Jean F. O'Barr, Sarah Westphal-Wihl and Mary Wyer, *Feminist Theory in Practice and Process* (Chicago: University of Chicago Press, 1989), p. 61.

53. Nell Nodding's otherwise impressive book contains no analysis of the effects on the moral agent of uncompensated caring. Nor is this a significant theme on the part of contributors to *Women and Moral Theory,* ed. Eva Feder Kittay and Diana T. Meyers (Totowa, N.J: Rowman and Littlefield, 1987), a book of essays on the philosophical implications of Carol Gilligan's research on gender differences in moral reasoning—research that has been a central source for theorizing about an

ethics of care. Claudia Card's "Gender and Moral Luck" in *Identity, Character and Morality: Essays in Moral Psychology,* ed. Amelie Rorty and Owen Flanagan (Cambridge, MA: MIT Press, forthcoming, 1990) is a notable exception. Two classic papers on the wrongness of female deference that present approaches somewhat different than my own are Thomas E. Hill, Jr., "Servility and Self-Respect," *The Monist,* Vol. 57, No. 1, January 1973, pp. 87–104; and Marilyn Friedman, "Moral Integrity and the Deferential Wife," *Philosophical Studies,* Vol. 47, 1985, pp. 141–150.

54. Teresa de Lauretis, *Alice Doesn't* (Bloomington, Ind.: Indiana University Press, 1983), p. 159. Cited in Linda Alcoff, "Cultural Feminism versus Post-Structuralism: The Identity Crisis in Feminist Theory," in Malson, O'Barr, Westphal-Wihl and Wyer, *Feminist Theory in Practice and Process* (Chicago: University of Chicago Press, 1989), p. 313.

55. On the necessity for coparenting, see Isaac Balbus, *Marxism and Domination* (Princeton, N.J.: Princeton University Press, 1982).

Index